Maintenance and Instruction Manual

G85CS · G80CS · P11
Scrambles Motor Cycles

NORTON VILLIERS LIMITED
NORTON MATCHLESS DIVISION

44, Plumstead Road, London, S.E. 18

First published — March, 1967

Published by
NORTON VILLIERS LIMITED,
Norton Matchless Division,
44 Plumstead Road, London, S.E.18.

INTRODUCTION

Welcome to the world of digital publishing ~ the book you now hold in your hand was printed using the latest state of the art digital technology. The advent of print-on-demand has forever changed the publishing process, never has information been so accessible and it is our hope that this book serves your informational needs for years to come. If this is your first exposure to digital publishing, we hope that you are pleased with the results. Many more titles of interest to the classic automobile and motorcycle enthusiast, collector and restorer are available via our website at www.VelocePress.com. We hope that you find this title as interesting as we do.

NOTE FROM THE PUBLISHER

The information presented is true and complete to the best of our knowledge. All recommendations are made without any guarantees on the part of the author or the publisher, who also disclaim all liability incurred with the use of this information.

TRADEMARKS

We recognize that some words, model names and designations, for example, mentioned herein are the property of the trademark holder. We use them for identification purposes only. This is not an official publication.

INFORMATION ON THE USE OF THIS PUBLICATION

This manual is an invaluable resource for those interested in performing their own maintenance. However, in today's information age we are constantly subject to changes in common practice, new technology, availability of improved materials and increased awareness of chemical toxicity. As such, it is advised that the user consult with an experienced professional prior to undertaking any procedure described herein. While every care has been taken to ensure correctness of information, it is obviously not possible to guarantee complete freedom from errors or omissions or to accept liability arising from such errors or omissions. Therefore, any individual that uses the information contained within, or elects to perform or participate in do-it-yourself repairs or modifications acknowledges that there is a risk factor involved and that the publisher or its associates cannot be held responsible for personal injury or property damage resulting from the use of the information or the outcome of such procedures.

WARNING!

One final word of advice, this publication is intended to be used as a reference guide, and when in doubt the reader should consult with a qualified technician.

CONTENTS

	Page
Technical data:	
G85CS and G80CS	5
P11	6
Routine maintenance	8
Running instructions	9
G85CS and G80CS engines:	
Lubrication	10
Engine service	14
P11 engine:	
Lubrication	23
Engine service	25
All models:	
Transmission	34
Clutch	35
Gearbox	37
Carburettors:	
Amal Monobloc — G80CS	41
Amal Concentric Type 930 — P11	42
Amal 5GP2 — G85CS	45
Front Forks	47
Rear Suspension	49
Wheels and brakes	49
Electrical systems	53

Foreword

The scrambler models described in this manual are precision-built machines designed to meet the requirements of the most exacting rider.

Although straightforward in design, they have been developed to a high degree of efficiency using the knowledge gained in tough international competitions.

In their construction only materials of the highest quality are used, manufacture and assembly being carried out by skilled craftsmen with the care and attention to detail necessary in the production of machines of this calibre.

Maintenance is reasonably simple and to ensure the utmost reliability the instructions contained in this manual should be carefully followed. Most of the servicing is well within the capabilities of the average rider, a feature which competition riders will appreciate, but where the necessary workshop facilities and specialised knowledge are not available it is advisable to entrust the work to a qualified repairer experienced in the preparation of competition machines.

When fitting replacement parts it is important to use components manufactured or approved by Norton Villiers Ltd. These are obtainable from any spares stockist but the full engine number must be quoted to ensure correct identification and prompt supply.

TECHNICAL DATA

Models G85CS and G80CS

	G85CS	G80CS
Engine number		Stamped on crankcase
Frame number		Stamped on right-side frame lug
Cylinder bore, finished size		3.385 in./3.386 in. (85.98mm/86.00mm)
Stroke		3.348 in. (85.5mm)
Cubic capacity		30.5 cu.in. (498 c.c.)
Compression ratio	12.5 : 1	8.7 : 1

Carburettor

	G85CS	G80CS
Type	Amal 5GP2	Amal Monobloc 389/12
Choke size	1 3/8 in.	1 3/16 in.
Main jet:		
with filter	290	270
without filter	310	—
Throttle slide	No. 6	No. 3
Air jet	.125 in.	—
Pilot jet	—	No. 30
Needle	5GP6	Central notch

Capacities

Gas tank	2.4 gallons (U.S.A.)
Oil tank	6 pints (U.S.A.)
Gearbox	1.2 pints (U.S.A.)
Front chain case	2.5 fluid oz.
Front forks	6.5 fluid oz.

Valve timing

Inlet valve opens	60° b.t.d.c.
Inlet valve closes	69° a.b.d.c.
Exhaust valve opens	74° b.b.d.c.
Exhaust valve closes	46° a.t.d.c.
Ignition timing: 12.5 compression ratio	33°/34° (.35 in.-8.9mm) full advance
Ignition timing: 8.7 compression ratio	38° (.432 in-10.98mm) full advance
Spark plug	Champion N57R

Gear ratios

	G85CS	G80CS
Top	7.5 : 1	5.8 : 1
Third	9.1 : 1	7.08 : 1
Second	12.7 : 1	9.85 : 1
First	19.1 : 1	14.85 : 1

Sprockets

	G85CS	G80CS
Rear wheel	54 teeth	42 teeth
Clutch	42 teeth	42 teeth
Final drive	16 teeth	16 teeth
Engine	19 teeth	19 teeth

Chain sizes

	G85CS	G80CS
Front	1/2 in. × .305 in. - 67 links	1/2 in. × .305 in. - 67 links
Rear	3/8 in. × 5/8 in. - 104 links	3/8 in. × 5/8 in. - 98 links

TECHNICAL DATA—*Continued*

	G85CS	G80CS
Torque-spanner settings		
Cylinder-head bolts		40 lb. ft.
Crank-pin nuts		240 lb. ft.
Valves		
Valve-spring free length between wire centres		$1\tfrac{11}{32}$ in.
Valve lift:		
Inlet		.442 in.
Exhaust		.399 in.
Spanner sizes (measured across flats)		
Rocker-box bolts		.445 in. and .525 in.
Cylinder-head nuts		.710 in.
Crankpin nuts		1.300 in.
Pump worm nut		.919 in.
Engine-sprocket nut		1.195 in.
Clutch fixing nut		.820 in.
Final-drive sprocket nut		1.480 in.
Rear-wheel axle nut	1.2 in.	.919 in.
Weight (dry)	310 lb.	399 lb.

Model P.11

Engine number	Stamped on crankcase
Frame number	Stamped on right-side head lug
Cylinder bore - finished size	2.8750 in. /2.8758 in. (73.025mm /73.045mm)
Stroke	3.503 in. (89mm)
Capacity	45.5 cu. in. (745 c.c.)
Compression ratio	7.5 : 1

Carburettor

Type	Amal 930 choke 30mm
Main-jet size (with air cleaner)	250
Main-jet size (with no air cleaner)	270
Pilot jets	25
Throttle slides	3
Needle jets	.107
Needle position	central notch

Capacities

Gas tank	3.6 gallons (U.S.A.)
Oil tank	6 pints (U.S.A.)
Front forks	6.5 fluid oz.
Front chaincase	8 fluid oz.
Gearbox	1.2 pints (U.S.A.)

Gear ratios

Top	4.42 : 1
Third	5.39 : 1
Second	7.52 : 1
First	11.32 : 1

TECHNICAL DATA—*Continued*

Sprockets
Engine   21 teeth
Clutch   42 teteh
Rear wheel   42 teeth
Final drive (gearbox)   19 teeth

Chain sizes
Front chain $\frac{1}{2}$ in. × .305 in. - 68 rollers
Rear chain $\frac{3}{8}$ in. × .380 in. - 100 rollers
Camshaft chain $\frac{3}{8}$ in. × .225 in. - 38 rollers
Magneto chain $\frac{3}{8}$ in. × $\frac{5}{32}$ in. - 42 rollers

Ignition timing   32° - 8.69mm (.343 in.)
Spark plug   Champion N4
Contact-breaker gap   .014 in./.016 in.
Tappet clearance (cold)-inlet   .006 in.
Tappet clearance (cold)-exhaust   .008 in.
Valve-spring free length (inner)   1.531 in.
Valve-spring free length (outer)   1.700 in.
Piston-ring gap (compression ring)   .014 in./.009 in.
Piston-ring gap (scraper)   .014 in./.009 in.
Push-rod length (inlet)   8.194 in. overall
Push-rod length (exhaust)   7.351 in. overall
Valve-head diameter (inlet)   1.500 in.
Valve-head diameter (exhaust)   1.312 in.
Valve-stem diameter (inlet)   .310 in./.309 in.
Valve-stem diameter (exhaust)   .310 in./.309 in.
Wrist-pin diameter   .6868 in./.6866 in.
Rocker-spindle bore diameter   .5003 in./.4998 in.
Rocker-spindle diameter   .499 in./.4998 in.
Wrist-pin bore in con rod   .6878 in./.6873 in.
Crankshaft-journal diameter (drive side)   1.1815 in./1.1812 in.
Crankshaft journal diameter (timing side) 1.1815 in./1.1812 in.
Crankshaft-journal diameter (con rod)   1.7505 in./1.7500 in.
Camshaft-bearing diameter   .874 in./.8735 in.
Camshaft bush (bore size)   .875 in./.8745 in.
Main bearing (drive side)   30mm × 72mm × 19mm
Main bearing (timing side)   30mm × 72mm × 19mm
Intermediate-gear bush diameter   .5625 in./.5620 in.
Intermediate-shaft diameter   .5615 in./.5610 in.

Torque-spanner loadings
Cylinder-head nuts   25 lb. ft.
Con-rod nuts   25 lb. ft.

Routine Maintenance

First 500 miles

Tappet adjustment	Check and adjust as required.
Oil tank	Drain and refill with fresh oil, clean filter in feed line.
Ignition	Check contact-breaker gap.
Gearbox (transmission)	Drain and refill with fresh oil.
Front-chain case	Check oil level with machine on both road wheels.
Steering head races	Check for looseness and adjust if required.

Every 1,000 miles

Oil tank	Drain and flush out tank and refill with fresh oil.
Rear chain	Remove for cleaning and greasing.
Gearbox	Take out level plug and check oil level.
Grease nipples	Use grease gun sparingly at all points.
Chaincase	Drain and refill with fresh oil.
Controls	Lubricate control levers and other small parts.
Front forks	Drain and refill with fresh oil.
Air filter	Change filter element according to track or road conditions.

Every 3,000 miles

Carburettor	Dismantle and clean.
Front forks	Check oil level.
Filters	Clean magnetic filter by removing sump plug.
Magneto	Adjust contact-breaker points gap.

Every 10,000 miles

Magneto	Have this instrument serviced.

Running Instructions

Gasoline

All models are fitted with high-efficiency engines which necessitate the use of 100 octane gasoline. The use of poor quality gasoline will cause detonation and subsequent damage to the engine.

'Breaking in' the engine

In the process of manufacture, selective assembly of such parts as the cylinder, piston and big-end assembly is used but it is still necessary to allow the moving parts to 'bed in' before subjecting the engine and gearbox to maximum stresses. On the care and restraint exercised during its early life depends the future performance and reliability of the engine.

During the first 500 miles the throttle opening should not exceed one-third of the twist-grip movement. Provided the engine is not allowed to labour the actual road speed is relatively unimportant. Full use should be made of the gearbox, not only to reduce engine stresses but to 'break in' the gearbox internals. Do not allow the engine to 'race' in the lower gears.

After the first 500 miles, the throttle openings can be progressively increased until approximately 1,000 miles have been completed. The machine should then be ready for use under race conditions.

During the 'breaking-in' period a certain amount of adjustment will be necessary as the components 'bed in'. Attention should particularly be given to such details as valve-rocker adjustment, chains, brakes, contact-breaker points, all of which are calculated to settle down during this period. Pay particular attention, too, to the steering head and frame races as undue movement in these bearings will damage the races. Movement can usually be detected by trying to push the machine with the front brake applied.

Gear shift

If at the first attempt the first gear will not engage, release the clutch lever and make a further attempt, when the gear will engage easily. This condition may exist with a new machine but tends to disappear with further use.

Always operate the hand clutch lever and the gear-shift pedal simultaneously with a steady pressure. Do not stamp on the gear-shift pedal.

To engage first gear, disengage the clutch by pulling the clutch lever towards the handlebar and raise the gear-shift pedal upwards as far as it will go and release it. Release the clutch lever slowly and at the same time open the throttle slightly, when the machine will move forward. To select a higher gear, operate the clutch lever and press the gear-shift pedal downwards as far as it will travel and release it. Repeat the operation to select the higher gears.

The clutch should only be used to change gear and to come to a standstill and should not be slipped to control road speed. Slipping the clutch unduly can generate heat which in time will weaken the clutch-spring pressure and reduce the efficiency of the clutch.

G85CS and G80CS Engines

Lubrication System

Dry-sump lubrication is used, oil being circulated by a gear-type pump. The feed and return side of the system is contained in one unit comprising four close-fitting gears in a cast-iron body. The gears used on the return side are larger than those used on the feed side, their greater capacity ensuring efficient sump scavenging.

Oil circulation

Oil flows to the pump by gravity, passing through a coarse-mesh filter in the tank end of the oil-feed pipe. A coarse filter is used to ensure a flow of oil when cold. In these conditions the engine should not be raced and should be allowed to idle for a short while until the oil temperature has increased sufficiently to give a full flow.

Oil is forced into the engine under pressure via a drilling in the timing cover, through a steel quill situated in the timing-side axle and emerges at the side of the crank pin to lubricate the big-end assembly. A restricted oil supply is by-passed through a union on the timing cover, to which a pipe taking oil to the rocker gear is attached. Oil is pumped back to the tank through a drilling in the crankcase.

Oil pump

The oil pump is attached to the crankcase by two studs and secured by two nuts. A heat-resisting conical-shaped rubber is attached to the oil-pump body to make an oil seal between the pump and the drilling in the timing cover. Pressure between the conical-shaped rubber must be maintained otherwise oil can leak under pressure instead of being forced to the big-end assembly.

Undue pressure on the conical rubber is not necessary as this would deform the shape of the conical portion. The amount of pressure can be checked by taking out the cams to allow the timing cover to move freely. With the timing cover in position the pressure on the rubber should only be sufficient to move the cover outwards by .010 in. Where a replacement rubber is not available shim washers placed between the rubber and the pump body will adjust the pressure as required. In the event of an oil failure this part of the system should be examined.

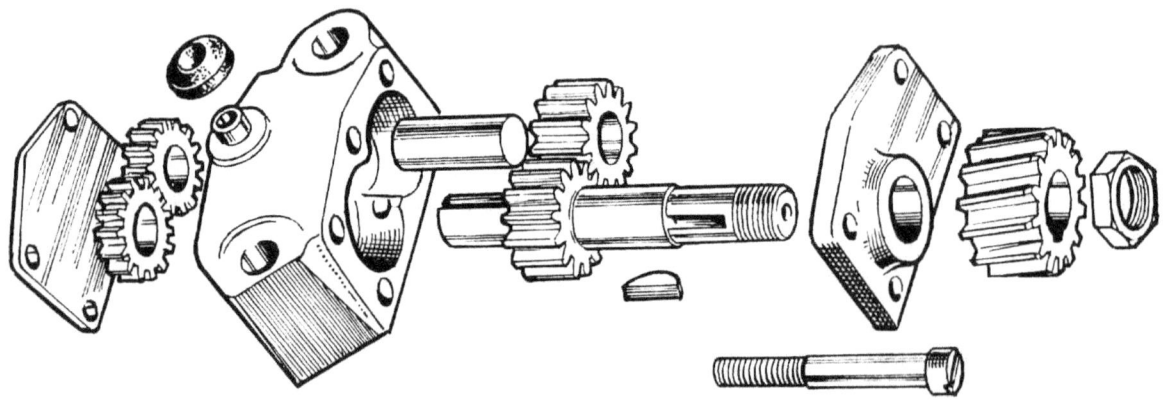

Fig. 1. Oil-pump components

If the pump body is dismantled care should be taken to ensure that the pump-body plates are flush with the body. Before refitting the pump body to the crankcase place a straight edge on the pump-body face where it butts against the crankcase to check that it is perfectly flat. If it is bowed, even slightly, an air leak will occur between the pump body and the crankcase and the return side of the oiling system will not operate efficiently. To remedy this rub the body on a face plate until it is perfectly flat, then flush out the pump until all traces of abrasive are removed. A slight smear of non-setting jointing compound on the body face will help to make an oil-tight joint. Do not use undue force when tightening the pump fixing nuts.

Check valve

A simple check valve (Fig. 2) is provided to prevent oil seeping into the crankcase when the engine is stationary.

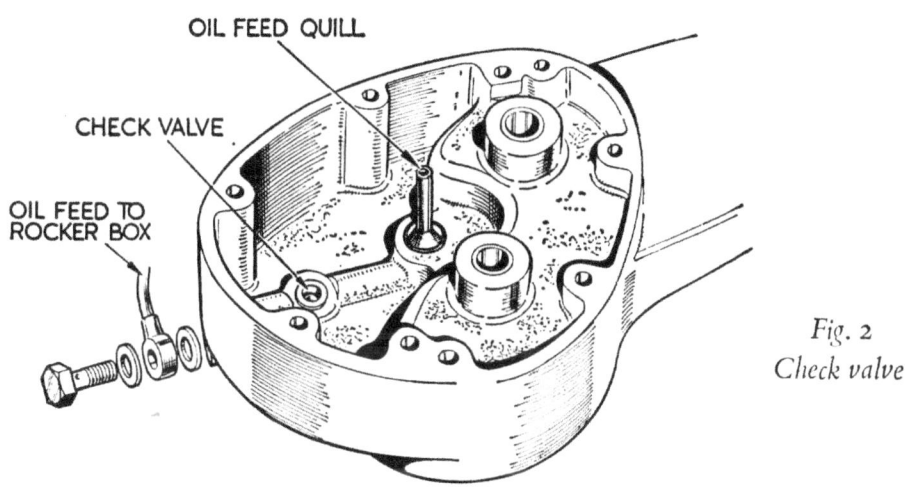

Fig. 2
Check valve

Adjustment of oil feed

With the exception of the oil feed to the inlet valve and guide, which is regulated by a needle screw situated in the cylinder head (Fig. 4), the internal oil flow is regulated by predetermined restriction in the oil drillings in the crankcase. The approximate setting of the needle screw is one-sixth of a turn from the fully closed position and once this is set no further attention is required unless the engine smokes unduly and the oil consumption increases, due to excess oil reaching the inlet valve and guide.

Crankcase pressure-release valve

This valve, consisting of a steel diaphragm on a serrated seat, will be found on the drive side of the crankcase adjacent to the engine main shaft. This is a simple flap valve and should not be disturbed unnecessarily. If the valve has been dismantled it is vital to ensure that the diaphragm lies in its serrated seat. A little grease will retain the diaphragm in position during assembly. If improperly located the diaphragm will become trapped between the seat and the crankcase and the valve will become inoperative. The oil pipe attached to this valve is connected to the oil tank.

Checking oil circulation

After removing the oil-tank filler cap oil will be seen emerging from the pipe in the tank as it is returned from the sump. When first starting the engine the flow of oil will diminish in volume as scavenging of the sump takes place. This is normal. If oil fails to return an immediate investigation must be made as this indicates that the system is not operating.

RECOMMENDED LUBRICANTS

Efficient lubrication is of vital importance and it is false economy to use cheap grades of oil. When buying oils or grease it is advisable to specify the brand as well as the grade and, as an additional precaution, to buy from sealed containers.

Engine

Ambient temperature above 32°F use S.A.E. 20/40 or straight S.A.E. 30 oil.
Ambient temperature below 32°F use S.A.E. 10/30 or S.A.E. 20 oil.

The following brands are recommended:
  Mobiloil
  Castrol
  Energol
  Essolube
  Shell
  Regent Advanced Havoline

Gearbox

Ambient temperature above 32°F: S.A.E. 50 or GX90
Ambient temperature below 32°F: S.A.E. 30

Hub and frame parts

  Mobilgrease MP
  Castrolease Heavy
  Energrease C3
  Regent Marfax
  Shell Retinax A. or C.D.

Teledraulic front forks

  Mobiloil Arctic (S.A.E. 20)
  Castrolite (S.A.E. 10W-30)
  Energol (S.A.E. 20)
  Essolube 20 (S.A.E. 20)
  Shell X-100 Motor Oil 20/20W (S.A.E. 20)

Rear chains

Mobilgrease MP
Esso Fluid Grease
Energrease A.O.
Castrolease Grease Graphited

Gearbox lubrication

Use one of the recommended grades of oil.

Oil is inserted through the filler-cap orifice located on top of the transmission cover. Do not exceed the specified amount as an excess will cause leakage and a break-down of the oil seals. Check the oil level every 1,000 miles and top up as required.

An oil-level plug is located near to the kickstarter axle and when removed indicates the maximum permissible oil level.

A screwed oil drain plug is situated at the rear end of the transmission shell for draining the gearbox when oil changes are necessary.

Chain lubrication

Use engine oil to lubricate the front chain which runs in an oil bath. To top up, place the machine on both road wheels and pour in sufficient oil to allow the lower run of the front chain just to make contact with it.

The rear chain, being exposed, must be lubricated at frequent intervals, using one of the recommended greases.

After prolonged use or where the machine has been operating in sandy or dusty conditions the chain should be removed and washed in kerosene and after cleaning soaked in one of the recommended greases, heated until it becomes fluid. Drain off the surplus grease before refitting.

If it is not convenient to remove the rear chain, use a Wesco gun to force the lubricant onto the joints formed by the rollers and side links.

Wheel-hub lubrication

The front hub on both models is packed with grease during assembly and does not require frequent attention. During a complete overhaul the grease should be changed. The journal bearings in the rear wheel are also prepacked with grease and provided there is no overheating of the hub, due to a too-closely adjusted brake or tight rear chain, no attention is needed until 10,000 miles have been covered, at which stage the grease should be changed.

Steering-head races

Grease nipples are fitted to the frame head lug for grease-gun lubrication.

General

Apply oil to all controls but use the grease gun sparingly on the nipples for the brake expander bushes to avoid contamination of the brake linings.

G85CS and G80CS Engine Service

Decarbonising

After considerable mileage, loss of power will inevitably result from a build-up of carbon in the ports, combustion chamber and on the piston crown. The power loss may be made more evident by weak compression due to burnt or pitted valves and valve seats.

With the cylinder head and valves removed clean off the carbon deposits with suitably shaped metal scrapers, finishing off with a soft brass-wire brush.

Examination will reveal if the valves and seats require grinding. If they are badly burnt or pitted, they should be refaced, using specialist equipment, before being finally ground in.

Valve grinding

Polish the valve throat and head and with a smear of fine grinding paste spread evenly over its face return the valve to its seat. Using a suction-type valve-grinding tool, rotate the valve to and fro, exerting light pressure. After every few strokes lift the valve and turn it through 180° before continuing.

At intervals, clean the grinding paste from the valve and seat and examine the work. Apply a fresh coat and carry on until the face and seat show a uniform narrow grey line around the full circumference. When satisfied, remove all traces of grinding paste with clean petrol.

Tappet (push rod) adjustment (Fig. 3)

The top push-rods ends have screwed extensions held in position by locknuts to provide adjustment, which should be made when the engine is cold. Because of the special cams fitted, it is most important that this adjustment is accurately made to obtain maximum performance. Position the piston on top dead centre of the firing stroke with both valves closed.

Fig. 3

1. Inlet rocker arm
2. Locknut
3. Cupped adjusting screw
4. Locknut
5. Adjusting-screw sleeve
6. Exhaust rocker arm

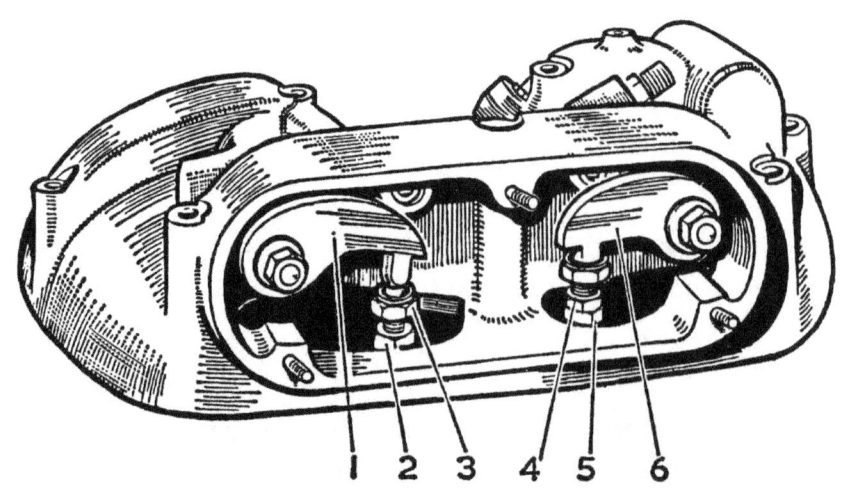

Inlet push-rod

Remove the three knurled nuts and washers and take off the rocker cover. With a spanner, hold the sleeve at the top of the push-rod (5), release the locknut (2) and extend or shorten the push-rod by moving the cupped adjusting screw (3) until the clearance is nil and the push-rod just free to rotate by finger application.

Firmly tighten the locknut (2) and recheck the adjustment.

Exhaust push-rod

With the piston positioned as previously described, adjust the exhaust push-rod to obtain a nil clearance, then unscrew the cupped adjuster (3) one sixth of a turn or one flat on the hexagon of the cupped adjuster. This will give the correct clearance of .005 in. Recheck the adjustment and replace the rocker cover. Undue force is not necessary when tightening the three fixing nuts as there is a rubber fillet in the cover.

Note: Adjustment should be made every 5,000 miles. The need for more frequent adjustment indicates that wear on the operating parts is taking place.

To remove gas tank - G85CS

Separate the gasoline pipe from the cock. Take out the bolt in the centre of the tank, which will allow the tank and the saddle to be removed.

To remove gas tank - G80CS

Separate the gasoline pipe from the cock, take out the two front-tank fixing bolts and detach the rubber band at the rear tank fixing.

To remove rocker box (both valves closed)

With the gas tank removed, take off the rocker-box cover as already described. Disconnect the pipe attached to the rocker box, remove the cylinder-head-to-frame steady stay, disconnect the valve lifter cable and remove the nine bolts securing the rocker box. Tilt the rocker box upwards and extract both push-rods. Mark the rods so they can be refitted in their original location. The rocker box can now be taken away from the engine.

To refit rocker box

Examine the rocker-box gasket, which must be faultless. If in doubt replace it with a new one. Clean the top of the cylinder head and the lower face of rocker box. Position the engine on the top of the firing stroke, with both tappets down. Put the gasket in position on the head.

Lay the rocker box in position, take up the push-rods, tilt the rocker box and insert the push-rods into the tunnels in the cylinder.

Insert the nine rocker-box bolts, with the bolt with the short head in the centre right-hand position, and the two bolts with screwed extensions in the centre at each side of the central short bolt.

Tighten all the bolts diagonally a little at a time. As a soft gasket is fitted undue force is not necessary.

Replace the cylinder-head steady stay and tighten the nuts firmly to eliminate excessive vibration. Connect the valve-lifter cable and the rocker-box oil-feed pipe, for which two spanners may be needed.

Check the tappet adjustment as previously described, lubricate the push-rod cups and refit the cover.

To remove cylinder head

With the gas tank and rocker box removed, take out the spark plug, take off the exhaust system and separate the air filter from the carburettor. Remove the carburettor. Unscrew the four cylinder-head sleeve nuts and remove the head from the cylinder, taking care of the two rubber seals encircling the push-rod tunnels.

To remove valve and guide

The valve springs can be taken away by inserting the index finger into the coil of the spring and giving a sharp upward pull. A sharp tap on the valve-spring collar will part the collar from the valve and expose the valve collets, which must be kept in a safe place. The valve can now be removed.

Both valve guides are a press fit in the cylinder head and are located by a circlip (Fig. 4).

Before taking out the guide, remove burnt oil or carbon from that portion of the guide outside the head.

Remove the circlip with a sharp-pointed tool or, if difficulty exists, by heating the head and tapping the guide upwards from inside the port to make the circlip more accessible. The valve-spring tool shown in Fig. 5 is part No. 018276.

The head must be heated to a temperature of between 150°C and 200°C before the guide is driven out. The guide must not be driven out with the cylinder head cold or the close fit of the guide in the head will be destroyed. Use a drift, or a scrap bolt with a small hexagon, to drive the guide down through the port in the head.

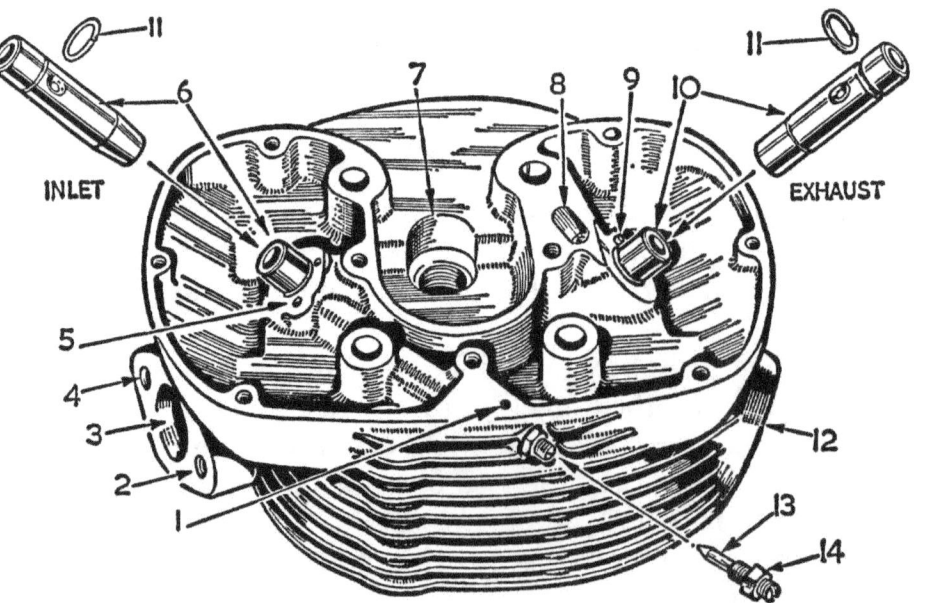

Fig. 4

1 Oil-feed hole
2 Carburettor fixing-stud hole
3 Inlet port
4 Carburettor fixing-stud hole
5 Dowel hole
6 Inlet-valve guide
7 Spark-plug hole
8 Oil-feed hole
9 Dowel hole
10 Exhaust-valve guide
11 Circlips
12 Exhaust port
13 Oil-feed needle screw
14 Locknut

Fig. 5

1. Valve collet
2. Valve-spring collar
3. Valve spring
4. Bolt
5. Valve-spring compression tool
6. Oil-feed hole
7. Oil-feed needle screw

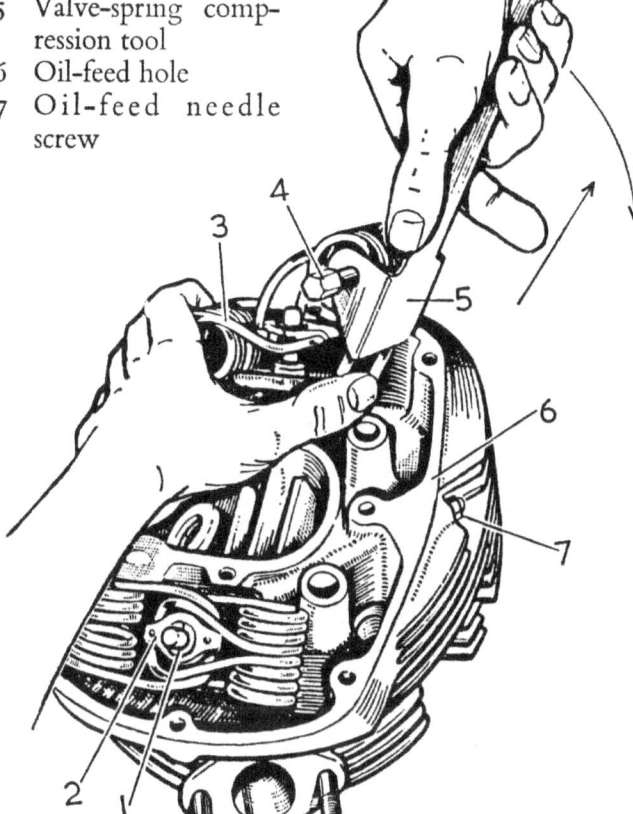

To replace valve and guide

Located properly, the oil hole drilled in the valve guide must line up with the oil hole in the cylinder head. Scribe a pencil line down the guide through the centre of the oil hole and line up the pencil marking with the centre of the oil hole in the cylinder head. Heat the cylinder head and press the guide into position. If the circlip is positioned first the guide can be pressed home against it.

To fit the valve pass a piece of clean rag through the guide, lubricate the valve stem and insert it into the guide. Pass the valve-spring collar over the valve, fit the collets, raise the collar and pull upwards to secure the collar. The valve springs can be fitted by hand, but the task is simplified by using the tool as shown in Fig. 5. When using the tool, anchor the spring into the collar, insert one of the rocker bolts through the coil of the spring and operate the tool as shown.

To replace cylinder head

There is no cylinder-head gasket, a gas-tight joint between the head and the cylinder being obtained by lapping the head onto the cylinder. A jointing compound must not be used as this would restrict the heat flow from the hottest part of the engine. Discoloration of the head or cylinder-joint faces indicates gas leakage, in which case the joint should be reground.

Make sure that the two top sealing rubbers are sound and are located in the recess in the cylinder. Place the head in position, fit the four stud washers and sleeve nuts and tighten them diagonally with a torque wrench set to 40 lb/ft.

To remove cylinder

Position the piston at the top of its stroke, raise the cylinder far enough to enable a clean rag to be inserted into the throat of the crankcase to prevent anything falling in, and lift the cylinder clear of the studs. Do not lose the two cylinder-base sealing rubbers.

To remake the cylinder-head-to-cylinder joint, smear a little fine grinding paste on the head face, take out the two top sealing rubbers from the cylinder and replace the head onto the cylinder. Using both hands, apply downwards pressure and with an oscillating motion rotate the head through 90 degrees until a perfect matt finish is obtained. Take care that all traces of grinding paste are removed by washing in clean petrol.

To refit cylinder

Before replacing the cylinder, examine the piston rings. If there is discoloration, indicating a gas leakage, fit new rings, first removing carbon from the ring grooves.

Fit a new base washer to the cylinder with jointing compound but use no compound on the crankcase side of the washer.

Make sure the clean rag is still in the throat of the crankcase before fitting the cylinder, as a precaution against anything falling into the crankcase. It is always advisable to use a piston-ring clamp to prevent ring breakages. If one is not available place the piston at the top of the stroke and pass the cylinder over the four studs, holding the cylinder with one hand and introducing the piston into the cylinder with the other while compressing the rings. With care the piston will easily enter the cylinder but before lowering it onto the crankcase remove the rag.

Removing piston

The piston should not be disturbed unless there is a positive reason for doing so. Take out one circlip with a rotary motion and from the opposite side press out the wrist pin, which is usually a light push fit. If the pin resists removal there may be a burr around the circlip groove which can be removed with a suitable scraper. A little gentle heat will assist removal. The piston crown is stamped 'FRONT' for location. The top piston ring is chromed to reduce cylinder wear, but two of these rings can be used if expense is of no consequence. The normal ring gap is .003 in. to .004 in. for every inch in bore size—nominal .010 in. to .014 in.

Take great care to locate the circlip in its groove after the piston has been replaced.

Checking ignition timing

Before the timing can be checked the contact-breaker gap must be set to .012 in. when fully open. If the gap has decreased it will have the effect of retarding the timing and conversely if the gap has increased it will advance the timing. The points should be adjusted with spanner 015023, which has a gap gauge attached to it. Alternatively, a .012 in. feeler gauge should be used.

Rotate the engine until the points are fully open.

Check the gap with the gauge, which if the setting is correct should be an easy sliding fit. If an adjustment is necessary release the fixed contact-plate adjuster screw with a screwdriver and alter the gap as shown in Fig. 6.

To remove contact breaker

Using spanner 015023, unscrew the hexagon bolt in the centre of the contact breaker, take out the bolt and pull the contact breaker away from the taper on the armature. When refitting, take great care that the key projection on the taper is properly engaged in the

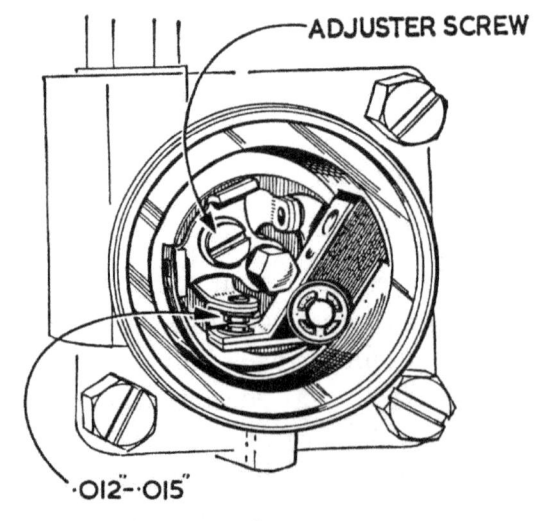

Fig. 6

armature otherwise the timing will be affected and the contact breaker will not run concentrically.

To retime ignition

Remove the spark plug and cable.
Remove the magneto-chain cover.
Remove the rocker-box cover.

Unscrew, one or two turns, the nut retaining the magneto-chain sprocket on the extension for the exhaust camshaft.

Using an old tyre lever, with one end bent at right angles inserted between the back of the sprocket and the chaincase, lever off the sprocket. If difficulty is experienced tap the shaft nut with a small hammer whilst applying pressure on the lever. The shock should separate the sprocket from the shaft. Rotate the engine until both valves are closed.

Insert a steel rod through the spark-plug hole and feel the piston by rocking the engine backwards and forwards until the piston is at top dead centre.

Mark the rod level with the face of the spark-plug hole. Make another mark to the measurement shown in the technical data **above** the mark already made.

Put the rod back into the cylinder and turn the engine slowly backwards until the second mark on the rod is flush with the face of the spark-plug hole.

Move the ignition control lever into the fully advanced position. Turn the magneto clockwise as seen from the contact-breaker end until the insulated pad on the contact breaker just makes contact with the ramp on the cam ring and the points commence to separate. The moment at which the points begin to separate can be determined by inserting a cigarette paper between the points. The paper will be gripped when the points are closed but if pulled lightly will be released the moment the points begin to open. Press the lower sprocket onto the shaft, give the sprocket a light tap to secure it onto the taper and tighten the nut. Recheck the timing.

If the cylinder head has been removed, the correct position of the piston before top dead centre can be readily determined before the head is refitted.

A more accurate method is to use a degree plate on the flywheel drive-side mainshaft. The ignition timing on the G85CS, with its compression ratio of 12 : 1, is critical and must be accurately set.

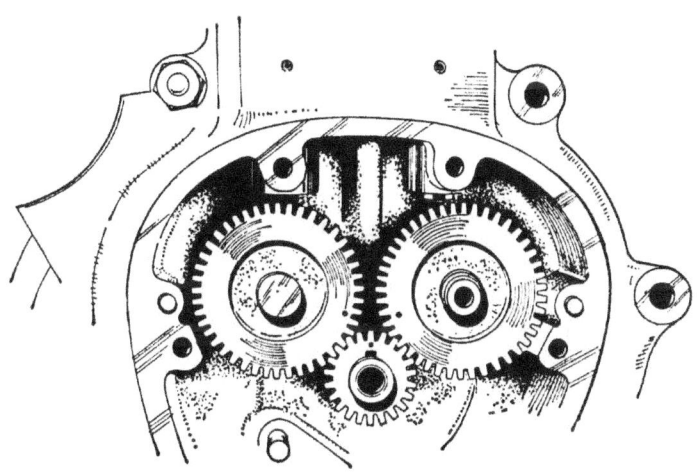

Fig. 7
Valve timing gear showing timing marks on camwheels and pinion

Valve-timing gear

The valve timing has been determined after considerable development and both cam wheels and the small timing pinion are marked for easy assembly (Fig. 7). No useful purpose will be served by deviating from the maker's markings.

To replace the cam wheels, first fit the inlet cam so that the mark on it registers with the mark on the small pinion.

Turn the engine in a forward direction about 20 degrees until the mark on the small pinion points to the hole in the crankcase for the exhaust cam.

Insert the exhaust cam so that its mark registers with the mark on the small pinion which, it will be obvious, is used for setting the valve timing for both cams.

The valve timing given in the technical data has been taken with the valve .001 in. off the valve seat in the head, using a cut-away rocker box with a mercer gauge in contact with the valve-spring collar to register the actual valve movement.

Tappets and guides

The tappet guides in the timing-side crankcase are a press fit in the crankcase and their removal is facilitated by two locating diameters in the guide housing $\frac{1}{4}$ in. at the top and bottom of the aperture. Both guides are located by an Allen screw which registers with a vee-shaped groove machined circumferentially on the outside diameter of the guide. As the tappet foot is larger in diameter than the hole in the crankcase the tappet must enter from inside the valve-gear chest.

Removing tappets

Tappet wear is negligible when regular valve springs are used and with adequate lubrication the need for replacements is rare.

To take out the tappets and guides, remove the cylinder head, the timing-gear cover and cam gear. Take out the two Allen screws which locate the guides, heat the crankcase and push both the tappet and guide until the guide is clear of the crankcase. The tappets can then be extracted from inside the gear chest.

To replace tappets and guides

Heat the crankcase, insert one of the tappets through the guide hole from inside the gear chest, place the guide over the tappet and press home until the vee-shaped groove registers with the Allen-screw hole. Tighten the fixing screw and deal with the other guide in a similar manner. Oil both tappets after assembly.

To remove timing cover

Take off the cover for the magneto chain (8 screws).

Release the nut on magneto armature fixing the top sprocket and separate the sprocket from its taper.

Take off the lower sprocket-fixing nut as previously described, remove the nut on the armature and remove the chain with both sprockets.

Take out the seven cheese-headed screws fixing the back cover and remove the cover from the crankcase.

To remove timing gear

Remove the two fixing nuts and pull the pump clear of the studs.

Remove the pump worm nut, which has a LEFT-HAND THREAD.

Take out the cam wheels from the crankcase.

The small timing pinion has a parallel bore and can usually be pulled off the shaft without difficulty.

Reassemble as described in the timing-gear paragraph.

Separating the crankcase

With the unit removed from the frame, strip down the engine as already described, up to dismantling the timing gear and removing the small timing-gear pinion. Take off the engine sprocket, which is on a splined shaft and can usually be extracted from the shaft without the use of an extractor tool.

Take out all bolts passing through the crankcase and tap one of the cylinder studs with a soft-faced mallet to separate the two crankcase halves. The inner race of the roller bearing will remain on the flywheel shaft.

If difficulty exists the crankcase halves can be parted by holding the assembly and striking the drive-side shaft against the top of a wooden bench. Watch for the spacer on drive-side shaft.

Removing roller-bearing inner race

The roller-bearing inner race is a press fit on the shaft and should not be disturbed except for renewal. To remove it, use two taper steel wedges between the sleeve and the flywheel face, taking care to avoid bruising, and tap the wedges until a gap is formed between the sleeve and the flywheel. A puller can then be used to extract the sleeve from the shaft.

To remove bearings from crankcase

The bearing housings in the crankcase for the two ball races have two diameters, that nearer to the engine sprocket having a close interference fit and that nearer to the flywheel a slight interference fit.

To remove the bearings, the crankcase must first be heated to prevent scuffing of the bearing housing during removal. After applying heat evenly around the bearing housing the bearings will fall out if the crankcase is dropped smartly on the bench. The roller bearing outer race can be removed in a similar manner.

Fitting ball bearings

The crankcase must also be heated when fitting the bearings. Press the outer bearing into the crankcase as far as it will go, line up the bearing spacer washer and press home the other bearing. Check that the inner sleeve of the ball race is free to revolve. If not tap the bearing out slightly to prevent end loading both bearings. It is for this reason that the outer bearing housing is a slight interference fit.

Note: Damage to the roller path on the bearing sleeve will be due to shock loading and not to normal wear and indicates that either the bearing sleeve is a poor fit on the crankshaft or the bearing outer ring in the crankcase is not a close fit in its housing. A close fit must be restored to prevent a repetition.

Flywheels

The flywheels are made from steel billets, the crankpin being dimensionally the same as that fitted to the G50 road racer. During assembly the flywheels are forced together under a heavy press to obtain a rigid assembly. If this equipment is not available no attempt should be made either to separate or reassemble the flywheels. Any attempt to assemble by simply pressing them together and relying on the tightness of the two nuts will cause the flywheels to flex under load and damage the bearings and crankpin.

Note: Shim washers are not used to adjust flywheel end play in the crankcase, the flywheels being pulled hard against the drive-side bearings when the sprocket nut is tightened. There is a spacer between the sprocket and the outer bearing.

Twin-Cylinder PII Engine

Lubrication

A table of lubricants is given on page 12. Details of routine maintenance for the single-cylinder models also apply to the PII machine. Where the machine is used for frequent short runs, however, the oil should be changed at more frequent intervals. During cold weather it is advisable, when first starting the engine, to run it at a fast tick-over speed to get rid of internal condensation.

Oil pump

A gear-type oil pump is operated by worm gear on both the pump and the timing-side shaft. The worm gears differ from those used on earlier '750' engines, being of the six-start type, which increases the pump speed and consequently the amount of oil circulating through the engine. The part number for the pump worm is 24733 and the shaft worm, 24732. If these gears are exchanged it is vital that the current type is used.

Oil circulation

Oil from the tank is fed by gravity and assisted by suction from the feed pump after passing through a coarse filter in the oil feed line. After passing through the feed pump, oil is forced under pressure through drillings in the crankcase and through the crankshaft to the engine. A by-pass from the oil feed conveys oil to the rocker gear via a pipe line from the timing cover, the supply being restricted by the fit of the two rocker spindles in the cylinder head. Oil drains by gravity through a drilling in the cylinder head and a mated drilling in the cylinder. The surplus oil and the spill from the timing gear drains into the sump, to be returned to the oil tank.

Checking oil circulation

To check that oil is circulating remove the oil-tank filler cap. After the engine has been stationary oil will drain into the sump and on starting the engine its return will be continuous and positive. As scavenging takes place the oil return will be spasmodic, the return side of the oiling system having double the capacity of the feed to ensure efficient scavenging. If oil fails to return the cause should be investigated without delay.

Oil filters

In addition to the filter in the oil feed line, there is another in the sump through which oil passes before going through the return side of the oiling system. This filter also acts as a drain plug, the hexagon of which measures 1.5 in. across the flats. The filter element is secured by a circlip which after removal permits the element to be extracted from the plug for cleaning. Ensure that the circlip is correctly located when refitting. To avoid damage to the hexagon use a close-fitting spanner to retighten the filter plug.

Oil-pressure release valve

This valve is located in the timing cover adjacent to the oil feed line to the rocker gear. It is set on assembly and needs no adjustment.

Removing the oil pump

Disconnect the tachometer-drive cable and take out the 12 timing-gear-cover screws. To break the joint between the cover and the crankcase tap the cover free with a soft-faced mallet. Unscrew the worm gear from the crankshaft (LEFT-HAND THREAD) and take off the two nuts fixing the pump to the crankcase. If difficulty is experienced in removing the pump, place a lever behind the worm gear and carefully prise the pump from the studs.

After assembling the oil pump ensure that the pump end plates are not proud of the pump body or an air-tight joint between the pump and the crankcase will not be made. It is equally important that the pump-body face is perfectly flat where it joins the crankcase or an air leak will result. This will prevent oil returning from the sump and cause over oiling. Check the face with a straight edge and if necessary rub it down with abrasive cloth wrapped over a flat surface and flush out the pump to remove any abrasive particles.

Checking oil pressure

The oil pressure can be checked with a pressure gauge with a scale reading of 0 to 100 lb. per square inch.

The gauge can be attached to the engine at the union on the timing cover which conveys oil to the cylinder head. The feed pipe can be removed temporarily for this test or, alternatively, a "T"-piece can be interposed in the feed line.

The normal pressure is a minimal 50 lb. per square inch.

Pump oil seal

A conical heat-resisting oil seal is attached to the oil-pump body and is located by the short steel sleeve protruding from the oil-pump body. When the timing cover is fitted this oil seal must be under pressure if a positive oil seal is to be made. If the seal is damaged or is not under pressure a leak will occur and the crankshaft will be starved of oil. If there is an oil failure this part of the oiling system should be investigated. When pressure on the seal is correct there should be a gap of .010 in. between the cover and the crankcase before the cover is tightened up. If this gap does not exist a new seal should be fitted or shim washers placed between the seal and the pump body to obtain the required pressure.

Timing-cover oil seal

A special oil seal is fitted in the timing cover, encircling the plain portion of the crankshaft and preventing leakage of oil which flows from the feed pump through a drilling in the timing cover before entering the crankshaft. Oil pressure in the seal cavity tends to make the seal more effective but if the seal is damaged or badly worn oil leakage is inevitable. This point must be investigated in the event of an oil failure.

Crankcase-pressure release valve

Access to this valve is only possible after dismantling the crankcase as the valve is housed in the drive-side crankcase at the end of the camshaft. The valve is timed and ported with the object of releasing positive crankcase pressure caused by the downward movement of the piston. Oil discharged in mist form is carried back to the oil tank by a hose. The valve consists of a stationary plate behind the camshaft bush and a ported rotary plate which engages with the end of the camshaft. A light spring ensures contact with the stationary plate. This valve needs no adjustment or attention.

Note: The rotary portion of this valve must be perfectly flat for it to function properly and must be renewed if damaged, or if the dogs are worn.

P11 Engine Service

Decarbonising

There is no predetermined mileage at which the engine should be decarbonised. The need to do so, is usually indicated by a loss of engine performance, together with an increase in fuel consumption. With modern high-octane fuels detonation, which normally indicates the formation of carbon deposit on the sphere of the cylinder head and on the piston crowns, is rarely audible and if the performance and fuel consumption are satisfactory there is no need to strip down the engine.

If there is a falling off in engine performance, however, the owner should first check the rocker clearances, spark plug, carburation and contact-breaker gap before disturbing the engine. It is possible that an adjustment will restore performance and eliminate the need to dismantle the engine.

To remove cylinder head

Have available the following items:
- Decoke gasket set.
- Socket wrench, $\frac{3}{8}$ in. Whitworth.
- Tubular box key for $\frac{5}{16}$ in. Whitworth.
- Spanner for the exhaust-pipe ring nuts, SHU/29.
- Tubular box key for $\frac{1}{4}$ in. Whitworth.
- Open-end spanner, $\frac{3}{16}$ in. Whitworth.
- Allen key, size $\frac{7}{32}$ in.

Begin by undoing the two front fixing bolts and removing the gas tank and the rubber ring for the rear tank fixing. Remove in the following order:
- Both exhaust pipes with mufflers.
- Two spark plugs.
- Head torque stay attached to the frame and head.
- Two banjo pins for oil pipes.
- Air cleaner.
- Take out five bolts on top of the head.
- Two nuts below the exhaust ports.
- Three nuts between the head fins.
- Lift the head from the cylinder.

When a composition-type head gasket is fitted the head will usually come away from the cylinder leaving the gasket attached to the cylinder. If difficulty is experienced break the joint by tapping below the exhaust port with a soft-faced mallet. Raise the head as far as possible, using one hand to hold the push-rods which are raised as far as possible. The head can then be tilted and removed. Identify the positions of the push-rods so they can be refitted in their original places.

Decarbonising the head

All traces of burnt oil and carbon should be scraped from both valve heads and from the combustion chamber in the cylinder head before the valves are extracted. This will prevent carbon chippings entering the ports and eliminate risk of damage to the valve seats. Valve grinding should be reduced to a minimum or the valve seatings will become saucer shaped and cause gas leakage. Have the valves refaced and the seats re-cut if they are badly burnt or pitted. The seat angle is 45 degrees.

Removing valves

With the rockers clear of the valve stems, a valve-spring compressor tool will close the springs to enable the valve collets to be taken off the valve stem. These are easily lost and should be put in a safe place. Check the valve-spring free length against the dimensions given in the Technical Data and discard them if the free length is reduced by $\frac{3}{16}$ in. or more. Take care of the heat-resisting washers under the valve springs.

Valve-guide removal

The four guides are a press fit in the cylinder head and the head must be heated before the guides are removed with the aid of a drift. If this is not done the interference fit will be impaired and the guide will become loose. For the same reason the head must be heated when refitting the guides.

Pistons

With both pistons at the top of the stroke, remove the carbon on both crowns with a suitably shaped soft-metal scraper. Take care to remove any carbon chippings that may have collected in the recess between the top land of the piston and the cylinder.

Cylinder removal

Undo the nine nuts securing the cylinder to the crankcase and raise the cylinder sufficiently to enable the nuts under the lowest fins to be removed. Raise the cylinder and insert some clean rag into the mouth of the crankcase to prevent anything dropping into the crankcase.

Rocker removal

The rocker spindles are a close fit in the head, which should be heated to facilitate withdrawal. Use a $\frac{5}{16}$ in. draw bolt with a 26TPI thread and about one inch long, together with a short length of steel tube with an internal diameter slightly larger than the outside diameter of the rocker spindle. By passing the tube over the bolt and screwing the bolt into the rocker spindle, the spindle will be withdrawn. Take care of the thin steel washer and the spring washer at each end of the spindle.

When refitting the rocker spindles take great care to position the spindle correctly so that the projections on the oval washer register with the slots in the spindle. (Fig. 8). The oil holes in the spindles should face outwards from the centre of the head.

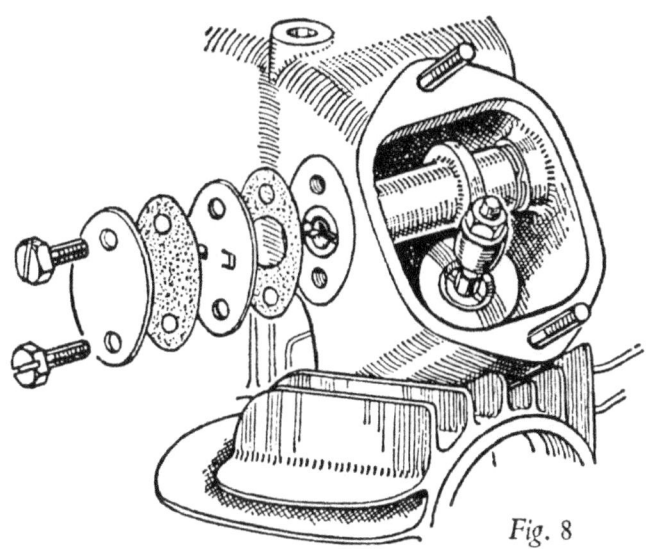

Fig. 8

Tappets

To remove the two split tappets, which are housed in the base of the cylinder, invert the cylinder, take out the wires and the screws to release the tappet division plates. The tappets should on no account be interchanged either singly or in pairs. The correct location is with the bevelled edges together, facing the front of the engine. Reversal will affect oil drainage from the head. Use steel wire to secure the plate fixing screws when the assembly is completed.

Piston and ring removal

The pistons are right- and left-handed, their location being stamped on the piston crown. They are also marked 'front'. The wrist pins are usually a light push fit. Pointed-nose pliers should be used to extract the wrist-pin circlip. If the pin cannot be pushed out gently heat the piston to facilitate removal.

Piston rings

Two compression rings and one special oil-control ring are used on both pistons. The top compression ring is chromed to reduce cylinder wear and must be used in this position. The second compression ring is a normal type. The special oil-control ring (Fig. 9) is used to prevent oil passing the piston and reaching the combustion chamber. It is essential that a duaflex ring is used because of the increased oil supply to the engine. A normal-type oil control ring will cause heavy oil consumption and spark-plug fouling.

Assemble the oil-control ring in the following order:-
  (i)   The corrugated expander ring;
  (ii) one of the rails;
  (iii) the wave spring;
  (iv) the remaining two rails. The one marked 'TOP' has a one degree taper face.

Do not expand the rings unnecessarily, but just sufficiently to pass the ring lands on the piston. No alteration to the ring gaps is necessary as the correct gap is allowed for during manufacture.

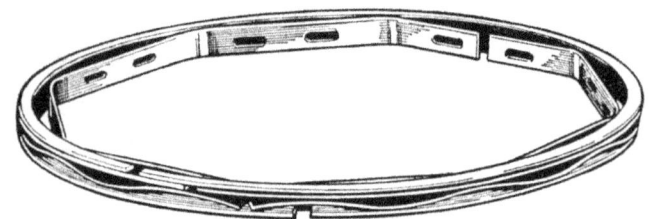

Fig. 9
Special oil-control piston ring

Refitting the cylinder

The use of piston-ring clamps is essential to enable the oil-control rings to enter the cylinder, especially if the work is carried out single handed. Both pistons should be supported as shown in Fig. 10, ensuring that both enter the cylinder without damage to the rings. Remove all traces of the cylinder-base gasket from the cylinder and the crankcase joint face. Use a new gasket, applying a little jointing compound to the base of the cylinder only. Check that the oil drain hole in the gasket registers with the hole in the cylinder and apply clean oil to both bores. Fit the piston-ring clamps as illustrated and engage the top lands of both pistons. A sharp push on the cylinder will force the cylinder down and dislodge the ring clamps, which can then be removed.

Fit the cylinder-base nuts, raising the cylinder to engage the nuts under the lowest fins. Tighten the nuts diagonally or there is a risk of breaking the cylinder-base flange.

Refitting cylinder head

Clean the top face of the cylinder and place a new gasket in position. Rotate the engine to position both pistons at the top of the stroke.

Place the head on the cylinder, tilt the head so that the four push-rods can be inserted into the tunnels in the cylinder, with the two longest rods in the midway position. Set the head square with the cylinder so that the push-rods engage in the cup portions of the tappets in the cylinder. The head will have to be lowered to do this.

Take up the two sleeve nuts used under the head, raise the head and insert the nuts

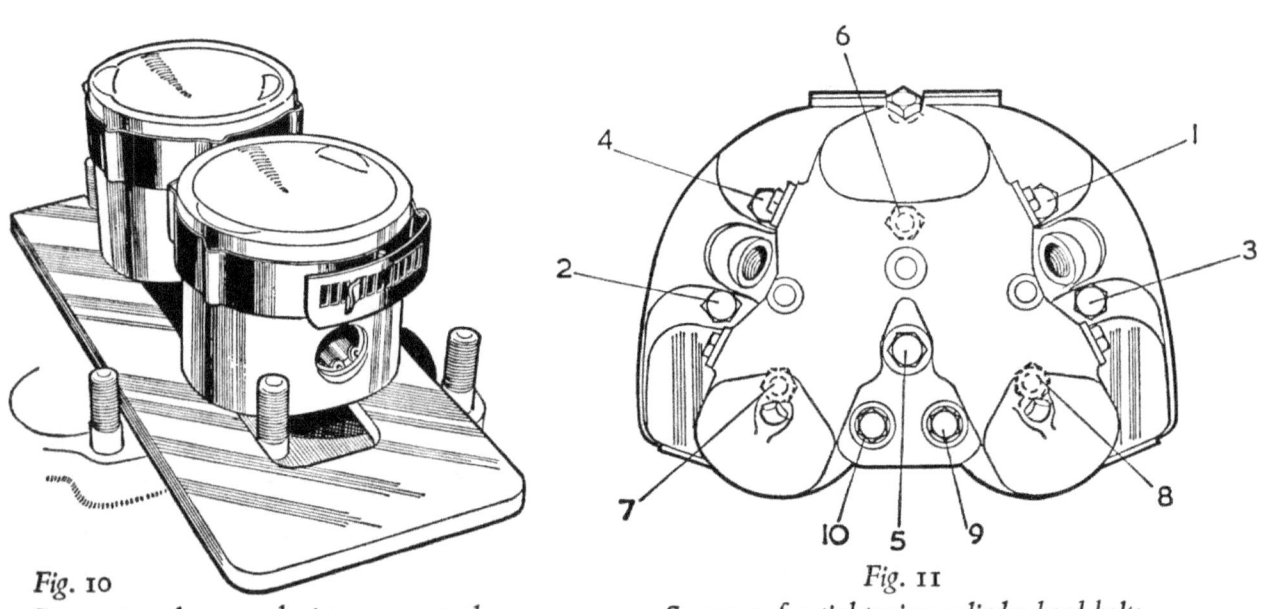

Fig. 10
Piston-ring clamps and piston-support plate

Fig. 11
Sequence for tightening cylinder-head bolts

28

between the head and cylinder to support it. Engage the push rods into the ball ends of the rockers, take out the sleeve nuts and lower the head into position. Fit the cylinder-head bolts and nuts and tighten in the order shown in Fig. 11. Use a torque wrench set to 25 lb./ft.

Rocker adjustment on cold engine

Have .006 in. and .008 in. feeler gauges available.

Deal with the inlet valves first by turning the engine slowly until the left-side inlet valve is fully open. Release the right-side inlet-valve rocker adjusting-screw locknut and with a spanner on the square portion of the rocker adjuster unscrew until there is clearance between the adjuster and the end of the valve. Place the .006 in. feeler gauge between the end of the valve and the adjuster and screw down the adjuster until it just nips the gauge. Tighten the locknut and withdraw the feeler. If the adjustment is correct the feeler will just slide through the gap between the adjuster and the end of the valve. Turn the engine again until the right-side inlet valve is fully open.

Deal with the left-side inlet valve in a similar manner. Adjust the exhaust valve rocker clearances in the same way as the inlet valves but using the .008 in. feeler gauge.

Reverse the sequence described for removing the cylinder head. Fit the torque stay from the head to frame and ensure that the fixings are tight. Run the engine for a short time and recheck the cylinder-head nuts. Recheck the rocker clearance when the engine is cold and finally fit the rocker covers.

Engine timing chains

The ignition-timing and camshaft chains are of short length and are not unduly affected by stretching, nevertheless correct chain adjustment is important to keep the timing constant. To adjust the camshaft chain, release slightly the two nuts fixing the tensioner slipper, which can then be moved as desired. The permissible amount of free movement measured in the centre of the chain run is $\frac{3}{16}$ in., but as chains do not always stretch evenly the movement should be checked in more than one place. Tighten the two tensioner nuts when the adjustment has been completed.

The ignition-timing chain is adjusted by releasing the studs fixing the contact-breaker unit, latitude between the studs and the unit enabling it to be moved. The free movement of the chain should be $\frac{3}{16}$ in. and again the adjustment should be checked in more than one place.

Checking ignition timing

For accuracy, use a pointer attached to some part of the engine and a degree plate mounted on the drive-side crankshaft, to record piston movement. Alternatively the piston movement can be measured before the cylinder head is refitted by using a straight edge on the top face of the cylinder and a short steel rule. The method of inserting a timing rod through the spark-plug aperture will be less accurate because of the steep angle of the spark-plug hole in relation to the piston crown.

First ensure that the contact-breaker point gap for both cylinders is between .014 in.

to .016 in. If the gap needs adjusting release the pillar nut (Fig. 12) that fixes the small plate with a screwdriver and with the screwdriver between the edge of the plate and the inside diameter of the contact-breaker housing move the plate in the required direction. Secure the pillar nut when the gap is correct.

Take out the left-side spark plug and the inlet-valve rocker cover. Rotate the engine until the left-side inlet rocker goes down and comes up again. The piston will then be approximately at the top of the firing stroke. Insert a short length of stiff wire through the spark-plug hole until it is in contact with the piston crown. Rock the engine backwards and forwards to determine when the piston is at top dead centre position and set the degree plate so that the pointer registers zero. Turn the engine backwards eight degrees on the degree plate, at which stage the points on the **top** contact set should start to separate.

A simple method of checking the point of separation is to place a cigarette paper between the points. The moment at which the paper can be withdrawn without tearing is the point of separation. Eight degrees on the degree plate is equal to .022 in. in piston travel. The ignition timing for the fully advanced position is given in the technical data. The timing given above is with the auto unit in the fully retarded position.

Note: If non-regular pistons are fitted, giving a higher compression ratio, the ignition must be retarded to prevent detonation.

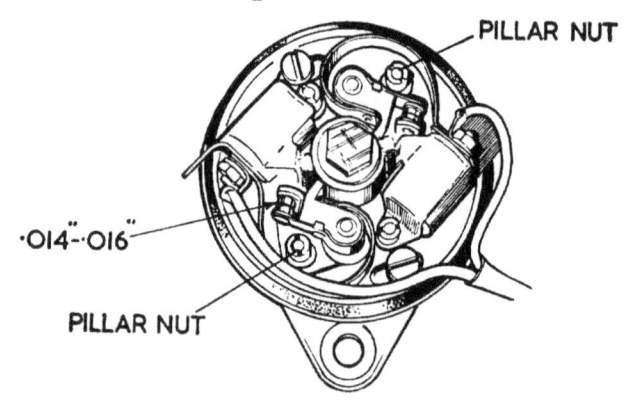

Fig. 12
P11 contact-breaker assembly

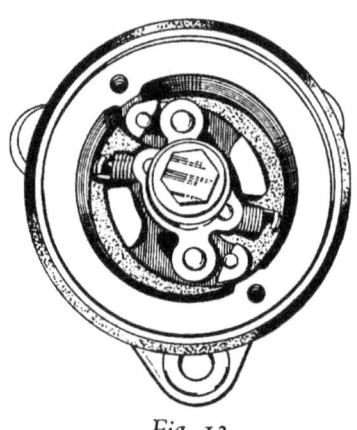

Fig. 13
Auto-advance unit

Adjusting ignition timing

Two slots in the contact-breaker base plate enable adjustments to be made, the plate being free to move on releasing the two cheese-headed screws. The contact-breaker cam runs clockwise looking at the contact breaker. To advance the timing move the base plate anti-clockwise and to retard it move the plate clockwise.

Removing base plate

To remove the base plate, take out the two cheese-headed screws and disconnect the two wires from the snap connector.

Ignition timing – auto-advance unit

The instructions on checking the ignition timing with the auto-advance unit in the retarded position are satisfactory provided the machine has not covered considerable mileage, in which case there is a possibility that wear will have taken place on the auto-unit limit stops. This would give a greater range of ignition advance if the ignition timing is checked or set with the auto unit in the fully retarded position. To check the timing in the fully advanced position take out the bolt in the centre of the contact breaker and, with a radio-type screwdriver in the slot in the outer edge, turn the cam clockwise to the fully advanced position. Details are given in the Technical Data.

Finding top dead centre

With the timing cover removed, the top dead centre position of both pistons can be decided by the position of the timing mark on the small pinion. If this is positioned at 12 o'clock both pistons will be on the top of their stroke.

Contact-breaker assembly

There are two sets of contact points with a separate H.T. coil for each cylinder. The contact-breaker housing is attached to the timing-side crankcase and houses the automatic timing control.

Note: If the contact-breaker plate or housing is removed the yellow and black wire attached to the top contact set goes to the left-side coil mounted on the rear-frame down tube. The H.T. cable from the left-side coil goes to the left-hand or drive-side cylinder. See electrical section for maintenance.

Refitting contact-breaker cover

Two insulated strips are attached to each condenser and are bent to cover and insulate the condenser terminals to avoid shorting out when the cover is fitted. Make sure that both strips are correctly positioned before fitting the cover. The cable entry is below the housing.

Removing drive sprocket

To remove the chain sprocket, which is a parallel fit on the contact-breaker shaft, push out the spring pin which passes through the sprocket and shaft.

To remove automatic control

The cam and automatic control can be withdrawn after removing the drive sprocket, cover and the two screws in the slots in the contact-breaker base plate. To remove the cam, take out the central bolt and with a draw bolt in the thread separate the cam from the taper shaft.

Valve timing

The small timing and intermediate pinions and cam-chain sprocket are all marked for correct assembly (Fig. 14). Six outer plates inclusively on the camshaft chain separate the marks on the intermediate pinion and the camshaft sprocket. The tooth gap on the intermediate pinion is marked with white paint and should engage with the tooth mark on the small timing pinion. The ignition sprocket and chain can be fitted when the valve timing has been set. When fitting the slipper-tensioner supporting plates the inside plate

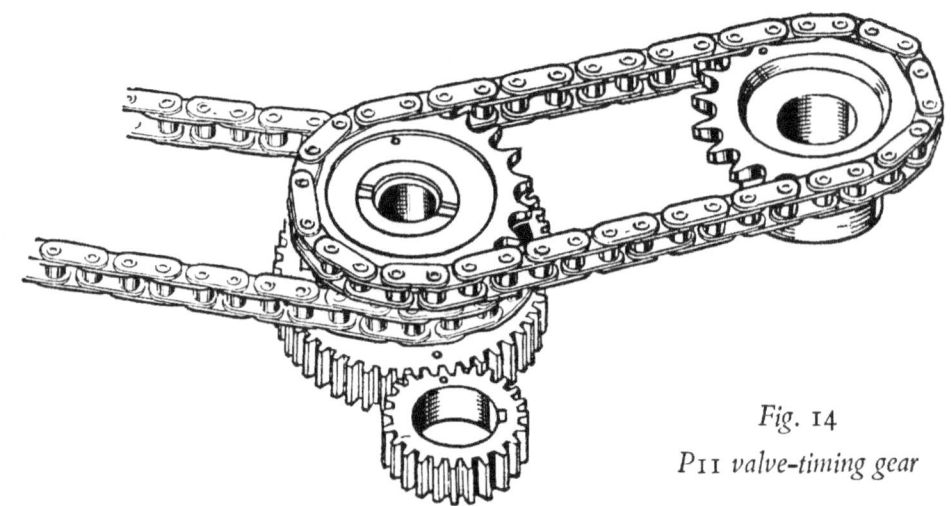

Fig. 14
P11 *valve-timing gear*

must be fitted with the long end (away from the hole) in the downward position. The outer plate is fitted with the long end upwards.

A cut-away timing cover is a useful aid when adjusting the timing chains and tightening the camshaft fixing nut.

Valve timing check with a degree plate

To check the valve timing have .016 in. and .003 in. feeler gauges available and open up the rocker clearance to .016 in. With the .003 in. feeler gauge between the valve end and the rocker, turn the engine until the rocker just pinches the feeler gauge. This will indicate on the degree plate the actual point of the valve opening or closing. The following figures are a mean reading taken from a number of engines:-

Inlet valve opens 50° before top dead centre.
Inlet valve closes 74° after bottom dead centre.
Exhaust valve opens 82° before bottom dead centre.
Exhaust valve closes 42° after top dead centre.

Reset the rocker clearances as already described.

Removing the engine

Take care to identify the locations of the various spacers when removing the engine bolts.

The engine and transmission can be removed as a unit. Start by following the details given to remove the cylinder head but leave the head in position. Disconnect the alternator and contact-breaker wires from snap terminals. Disconnect the battery wires for safety, undo the tachometer cable and oil pipes attached to the engine. Remove the outer portion of the front chaincase (14 screws) and carefully guide the alternator wires through the rear of the chaincase.

Take off the rotor, engine sprocket, clutch assembly and primary chain and remove the rear chain connecting link. Remove the rear portion of the front chaincase (3 screws) and crankcase shield. Take out all bolts passing through engine and frame.

Lift the unit from the frame, taking off the coils for more clearance if necessary.

Engine strip down

Lift off the cylinder head and remove the cylinder block secured by seven large and two small nuts.

Remove both pistons.

Take off timing cover (12 screws), tapping the cover lightly with a soft mallet and pull on the tachometer drive to break the joint.

Undo the two nuts and remove the oil pump.

Remove the oil-pump worm nut (LEFT-HAND THREAD).

Remove the chain-tensioner slipper, noting the way the plates are fitted.

Remove the camshaft-sprocket nut.

Remove the small timing pinion.

Remove the spring pin through the ignition timing chain and pull off the camshaft sprocket together with both chains and intermediate sprocket.

Pull off the timing pinion and remove the star washer and oil seal.

Remove the key in the drive-side shaft, the short bolt in the crankcase and the two screws at the bottom of the crankcase. Rotate the crankshaft until both con rods are at the bottom of the stroke. Hold the assembly with both hands and strike the drive-side shaft once or twice on a wooden bench to part the crankcase halves. Take out the camshaft and rotary breather valve and spring.

The timing-side ball race is a close interference fit.

Removing roller bearing

When the crankcase is separated the inner-bearing race usually remains on the shaft, leaving the outer race in the case. To extract the outer race heat the crankcase and drop it on the bench to free the roller race.

Removing ball bearing

Heat the crankcase around the bearing and drop it on the bench to free the bearing. Undue heat can loosen the intermediate-pinion shaft.

Checking the roller bearing

The roller path can be checked by using an open-end spanner with one jaw against the inner part of one of the rollers and the back against the crankshaft to prise out the roller, exposing the roller path. Turn the bearing so that the entire roller path can be examined. Use two wedges between the bearing and the crankshaft to make a gap and a puller can then be used to remove the bearing from the shaft.

Crankshaft assembly

After considerable mileage or if any part of the engine is damaged the crank cheek should be parted from the flywheel to enable the cavity in the shaft to be cleaned out.

Without experience and good workshop facilities, however, work on this part of the engine is best left to a competent mechanic. The crankshaft and journal diameters are given in the Technical Data.

Transmission - all models

Front-chain adjustment

Provided the oil level is maintained and the adjustment is correct long life can be expected from the chain.

The maximum free play measured from the centre of the chain run is ⅜ in. Check the chain in several positions as it may have stretched unevenly. The method of adjusting the front chain is shown in Fig. 15, with the exception that two adjusters are used on the G80CS model. To adjust the chain slacken the bolt (5) and release the adjusting-bolt locknuts (3).

Slacken the bolts (1) in the crosshead (2) to take up the slack in the chain. When making the adjustment pull or press lightly with the foot on the rear chain. Manipulate the two bolts (1) evenly until the correct adjustment has been reached. Tighten the nuts (3) and bolt (5).

Check the rear-chain adjustment as any movement of the gearbox also affects the rear-chain adjustment.

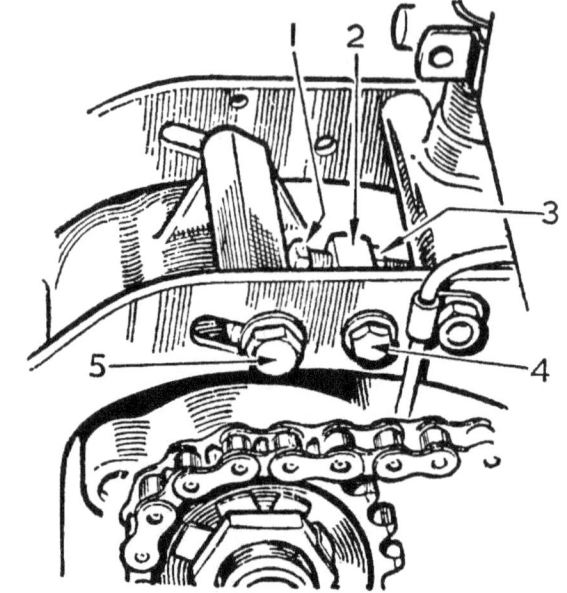

Fig. 15
Front-chain adjustment

Rear-chain adjustment

The fork ends of the swinging arm are slotted to enable the rear wheel to be moved either way to obtain correct chain adjustment.

Release the wheel spindle nuts and move the rear-wheel adjusters an equal amount to maintain wheel alignment.

Release the torque-stay nut on the G85CS to enable the wheel to be moved. The nut must be firmly tightened after adjustment.

Check the rear-brake adjustment after moving the rear wheel.

Magneto chain

The magneto platform hinges on one of its fixing bolts, providing ample movement for the adjustment of the magneto.

Take off the chain cover, slacken the nut on the rear bolt supporting the platform and with a screwdriver inserted under the platform lever upwards to tighten the chain. The correct free movement of the chain is ¼ in.

Tighten the platform bolt, grease the chain and refit the cover.

Front-chain case - G80CS and P11

The stator for the alternator is bolted to the outer part of the front-chain case. Attached to the stator is a cable, which passes through the rear part of the case. When removing the outer part, avoid strain on the cable. Snap connectors are fitted behind the rear part so that the case can be removed.

Clutch - all models

Removing clutch cable

Remove the oil-filler cap from the kickstarter cover and screw down the adjuster as far as possible on the clutch cable.

Take out the clutch inner wire from the slotted lever and disconnect the inner wire at the handlebar end and remove the cable clips from the frame.

Clutch-cable adjustment

A study of the clutch assembly (Fig. 16) will show the method of separating the clutch when the lever is operated.

To enable the clutch to operate satisfactorily there must be a little free movement between the operating lever and the long push-rod in addition to the $\frac{1}{8}$ in. to $\frac{1}{4}$ in. of free play in the clutch cable. To ensure that this free movement exists slacken off the cable adjuster as far as possible and take off the filler cap. With the index finger move the lever to and fro to indicate whether or not there is a slight amount. If there is no movement release the nut (B) on the clutch housing at the opposite end of the gearbox mainshaft and turn the screw (C) gently clockwise until it just touches the push-rod, then unscrew it half a turn only. Hold the screw in this position and tighten the locknut (B). Unscrew the clutch-cable adjuster, leaving $\frac{1}{8}$ in. to $\frac{1}{4}$ in. of free movement between the cable outer casing and the adjuster.

Clutch-springs adjustment

When the clutch springs are correctly assembled the end of the stud in the centre of the spring is just level with the face of the adjusting screw. The clutch is more than adequate for the power developed and no additional pressure on the clutch springs is, therefore, needed. If clutch slip is experienced, check the cable adjustment. When new the free length of the clutch springs is $1\frac{25}{32}$ in.

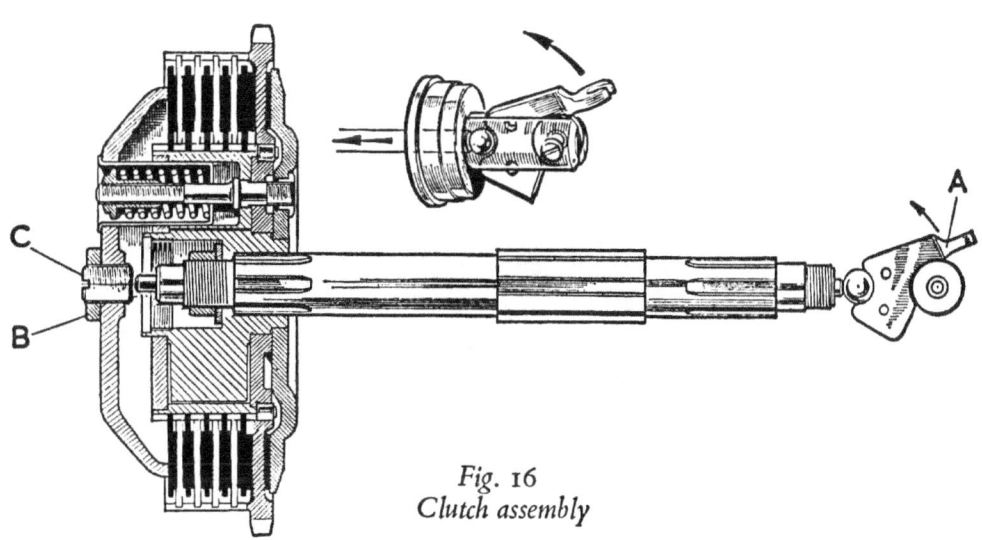

Fig. 16
Clutch assembly

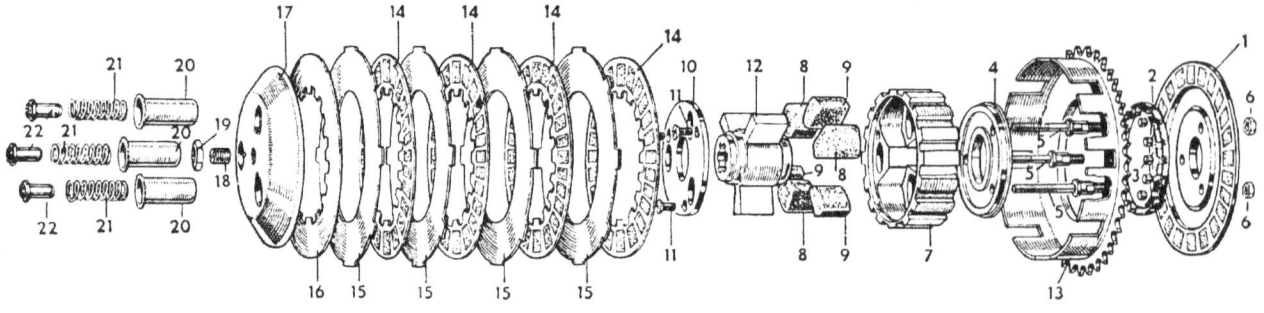

Fig. 17
Clutch components

Key to Fig. 17

1. Back plate (bonded)
2. Roller cage
3. Rollers (15)
4. Race plate
5. Spring studs
6. Spring-stud nuts
7. Centre hub
8. Shock rubbers (large)
9. Shock rubbers (small)
10. Shock plate
11. Shock-plate screws
12. Shock centre
13. Sprocket
14. Friction plates (double)
15. Steel plates
16. Friction plate (single)
17. Pressure plate
18. Pressure-plate adjuster
19. Pressure-plate-adjuster nut
20. Spring cups
21. Springs
22. Spring adjusting nuts

Dismantling shocker absorber

Three thin and three thick rubbers are housed in the clutch centre and are located by the clutch hub steel plate (Fig. 17). For access, take out the three screws and move the plate to enable a screwdriver to be used to prise out the plate (Fig. 18). To take out the rubbers use a "C" spanner to turn the hub and compress the thick rubbers, which will come out easily after the thin ones have been extracted.

Clutch bearing

The clutch hub is secured to the steel back plate by three spring studs and locknuts. After separating the back plate from the hub the bearing can be removed. When replacing, apply a little anti-centrifuge grease to the bearing.

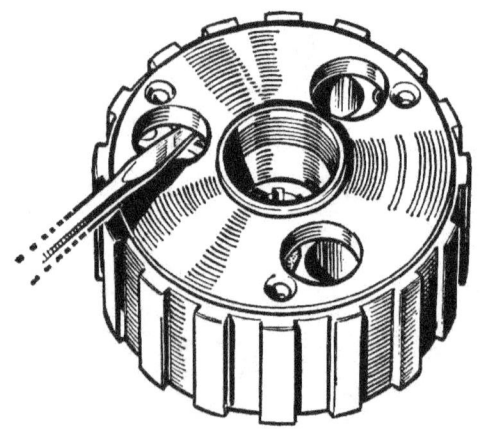

Fig. 18
Removing clutch cover plate

Gearbox - all models

The numbers mentioned in this section refer to those shown in Fig. 19.

Removal of outer cover (56)

Remove the drain plug (15) and drain off the oil.
Remove the inspection cap (66) and take out the cable from the clutch lever.
Remove the indicator bolt (62) but leave the pedal in position.
Remove the kickstarter bolt (90) and take off the crank.
Remove the five cheese-headed screws (68) securing the outer cover.
Remove the cover by pulling on the gear-change pedal.

Removal of inner cover (47)

Remove the ratchet plate and spindle (50).
Remove the clutch operating arm and roller (82).
Remove the lock ring (80), clutch operating body (79) and ball (78).
Remove the mainshaft nut (76).
Remove the seven cover-securing nuts (89).
Remove the cover, tapping the rear free from the dowel pins.

Removing gearbox internals

Remove the mainshaft first-gear pinion (39).
Unscrew and remove the selector-fork shaft (25).
Remove the forks (33 and 34).
Remove the clutch push-rod (21).
Remove the mainshaft (11) with the gears on the shaft.
Remove the layshaft (12) with the gears on the shaft by rocking the shaft sideways.

Removing cam plate (26)

Remove the dome nut (20), together with the complete plunger (18) and spring (19).
Remove the two bolts (28 and 29) over the plunger housing.
Remove the cam plate (26) with the quadrant (31).

Removing sleeve gear (23)

Remove the screw fixing the lock plate (4).
Remove the sprocket nut (5), which has a LEFT-HAND THREAD, using a close-fitting spanner.
Remove the sprocket (6) from the sleeve gear. This is on a splined shaft.
Remove the sleeve gear by tapping it through the bearing.

Removing sleeve-gear bushes

Note the location and spacing of the sleeve-gear bushes before pressing them out and take care when replacing them as they are the brittle oilite type.

Removing sleeve-gear bearing (17)

Prise out the oil seal (16) and its steel sleeve.
Heat the gearbox shell and drift out the bearing.

Key to Fig. 19

1. Clutch retaining nut
2. Washer
3. Locking screw
4. Locking plate
5. Locking nut
6. Drive sprocket
7. Gearbox shell
8. Stud (short)
9. Bush
10. 'O' ring
11. Mainshaft
12. Layshaft
13. Stud (long)
14. Washer
15. Drain plug
16. Sleeve-gear oil seal
17. Main gear ball race
18. Index plunger
19. Spring
20. Domed nut
21. Clutch push rod
22. Layshaft ball race
23. Main gear
24. Mainshaft third gear
25. Selector-fork shaft
26. Cam plate
27. Washer
28. Bolt
29. Bolt
30. Washer
31. Quadrant
32. Roller
33. Selector fork
34. Selector fork
35. Mainshaft second gear
36. Layshaft small pinion
37. Layshaft third-gear pinion
38. Layshaft second-gear pinion
39. Mainshaft first-gear pinion
40. Layshaft first-gear pinion
41. Kickstart pawl
42. Plunger
43. Pin
44. Spring
45. Axle
46. Gasket
47. Inner cover
48. Gasket
49. Gear-change spindle bush
50. Ratchet plate and spindle
51. 'O' ring
52. Pawl carrier
53. Washer
54. Return spring
55. Stop plate
56. Outer cover
57. Foot-change lever
58. Rubber
59. Indicator
60. Foot-change-lever bolt
61. Indicator washer
62. Indicator fixing bolt
63. Foot-change-lever washer
64. Nut
65. Inspection-cover screw
66. Inspection cover
67. Gasket
68. Outer-cover screw
69. Kickstart 'O' ring
70. Bush
71. Return spring
72. Stop-plate washer
73. Stop-plate screw
74. Circlip
75. Mainshaft ball race
76. Mainshaft nut
77. Kickstart-axle bush
78. Clutch operating ball
79. Clutch operating body
80. Lockring
81. Clutch-roller nut
82. Operating lever
83. Roller
84. Sleeve
85. 2 B.A. screw
86. Oil level-plug washer
87. Oil-level plug
88. Foot-change-pawl spring
89. Nut
90. Kickstart bolt
91. Kickstart crank
92. Pawl carrier 'O' ring
93. Pawl carrier bush
94. Kickstart axle stop
95. Kickstart axle cam
96. Kickstart axle cam rivet
97. Footchange pawl

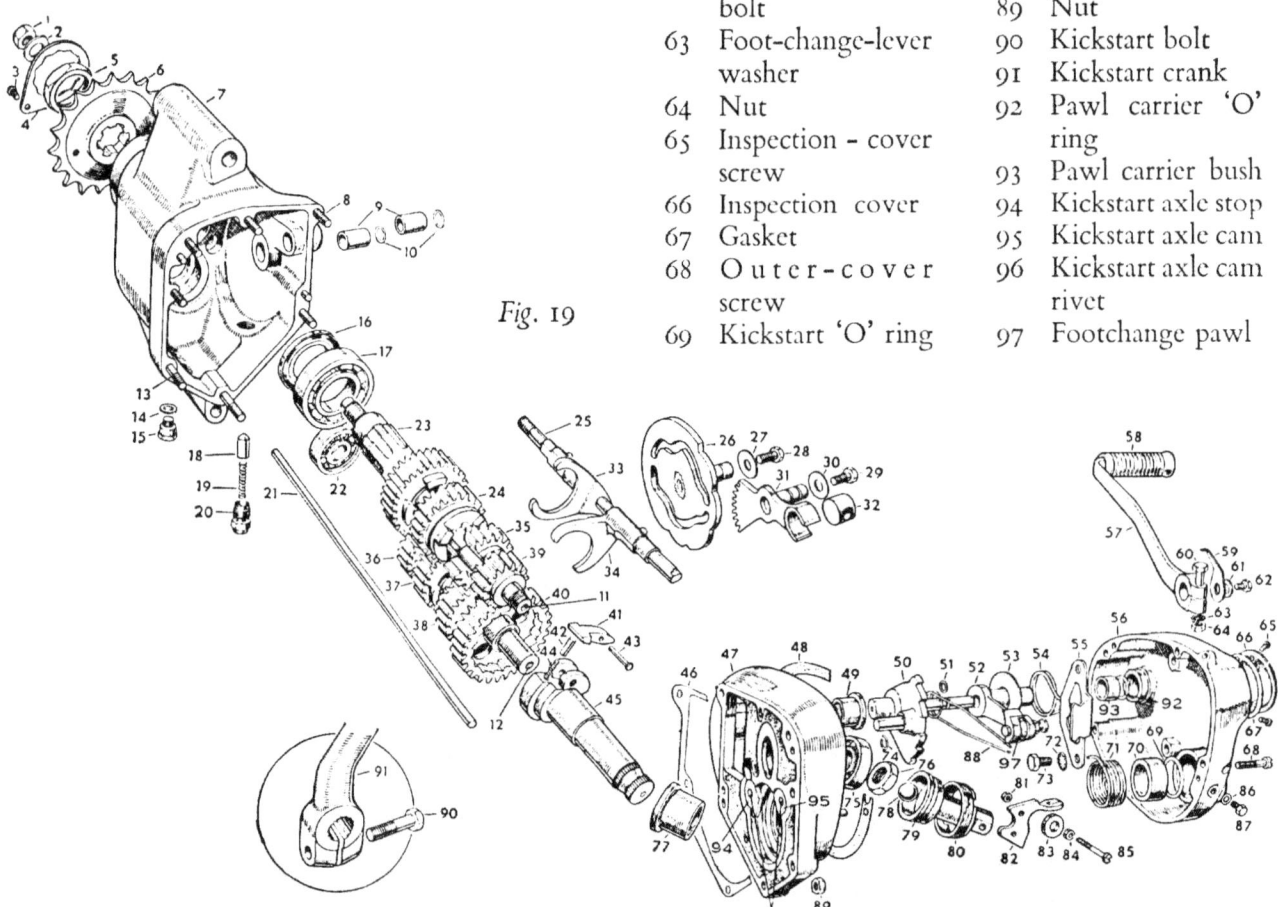

Fig. 19

Assembling the gear cluster

Introduce the mainshaft (11) through the sleeve gear and fit the third gear (24). Fit the second-gear pinion (35) with the striker fork (33) in the pinion groove and insert the projection of the fork into the groove in the cam plate (26). Fit the first gear (39).

To assemble the layshaft fit the fixed gear (36), third gear (37) and second gear (38), with the striker fork (34) in the slot for the second-gear pinion.

Insert the projection on striker into the cam plate slot (26), with the layshaft in the bush. Line up the holes in the two striker forks, pass through the spindle (25) and firmly tighten with a spanner on the two flats. Fit the first gear (40).

To complete the assembly insert the roller (32) into the quadrant (31) to take the spindle for the gear shift.

Fit a new gasket to the inner cover.

To ensure a straight pull for the cable, make sure that the clutch body is in line to take the cable before tightening the body lock ring (80).

Fit the outer cover, which should go into position without difficulty. If not, check and position the kickstarter pawl. Tighten the screws and fill the gearbox with a pint of oil.

Replacing gear-shift spring

Take off the outer cover and remove the ratchet plate and spindle (50), with the pawl spring behind it. Tap out the pawl carrier (52), together with its washer (53), remove the two bolts (73) and lift away the plate. The pedal spring correctly located is shown in Fig. 20.

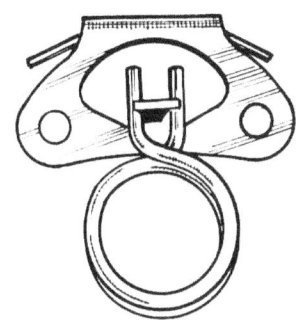

Fig. 20
Gear-shift pawl spring

Gear-shift pawl spring

If difficulty exists in selecting any gear, check the pawl spring (Fig. 21). If the spring is bent or damaged the pawl will not trip to select the gear and a new spring must be used.

The spring must be fitted with the straight leg in the uppermost position as illustrated. Make sure that the legs of the spring are on each edge of the pawl to enable it to trip and engage with the ratchet plate.

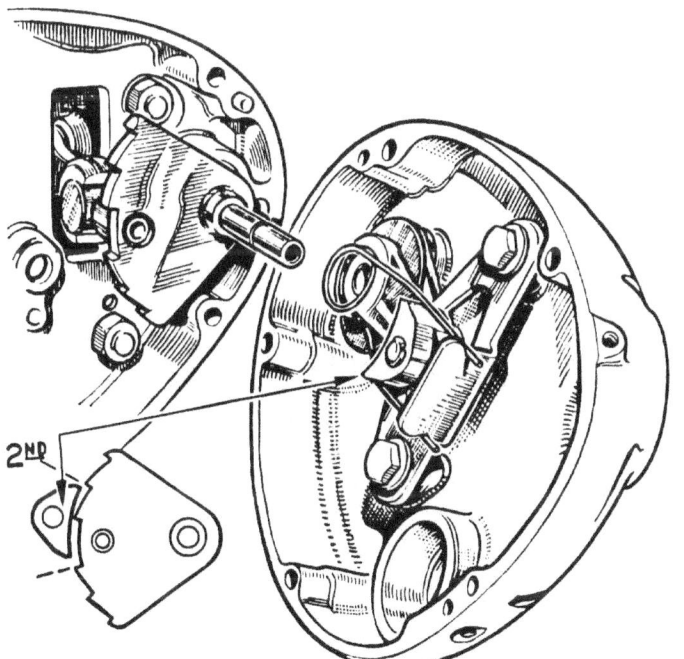

Fig. 21
Gear-shift mechanism

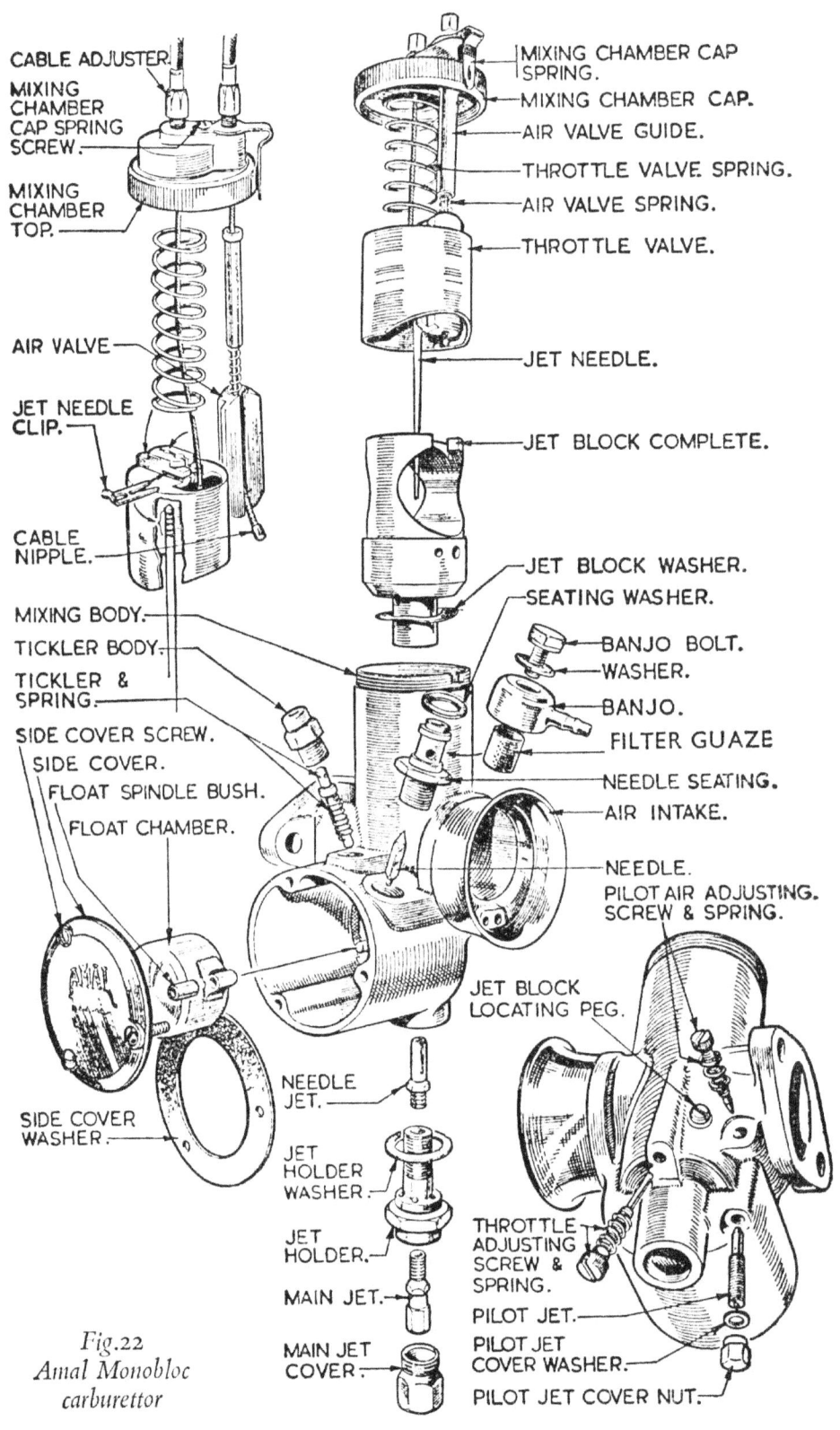

Fig. 22
Amal Monobloc carburettor

Carburettors

Amal Monobloc - G80CS

The Amal Monobloc carburettor fitted to this model is shown in Fig. 22. The main-jet size shown in the technical data is used when a muffler and air cleaner are fitted. If the muffler alone is removed use a 330 main jet. If both air cleaner and muffler are removed the jet size should be increased to 440. These jet sizes have been determined after careful tests but may have to be altered slightly to suit varying atmospheric conditions.

The main jet is accessible when the hexagon cover nut at the base of the mixing chamber is removed. The pilot jet is screwed into the carburettor body and protected by a small hexagon cover nut. Both jets are detachable and should be cleaned by using compressed air. Never use a pin or a piece of wire, otherwise the finely calibrated bore may be damaged. To remove the float, detach the float-chamber cover plate which is secured by three small screws. The float and float needle can then be taken out.

To remove the throttle slide, air slide and taper needle, unscrew the mixing-chamber knurled top ring. The needle is secured to the throttle slide by a spring clip located in one of the grooves at the top of the needle. As the throttle is opened and closed the taper needle moves up and down inside the bore of the needle jet, which is screwed into the jet holder at the base of the mixing chamber.

The phases of tuning the Amal needle jet carburettor are shown in Fig. 23, but before tuning ensure that the engine is in in sound mechanical condition and that the ignition timing and contact-breaker points gap are correctly set.

1. **Main jet with throttle fully open.** If at full throttle slightly closing the throttle or air control seems to improve power, the main jet is too small. If the engine runs "heavily" the main jet is too large.
2. **Pilot jet - with throttle up to $\frac{1}{8}$ in. open.** Close the throttle, allow the engine to idle fairly fast and set the ignition lever to the best idling position.

Screw out the throttle adjusting screw until the engine runs slower and begins to falter then screw the pilot-jet adjusting screw in or out until the engine runs evenly. If the idling speed is not too fast, regulate it by means of the throttle adjusting screw.

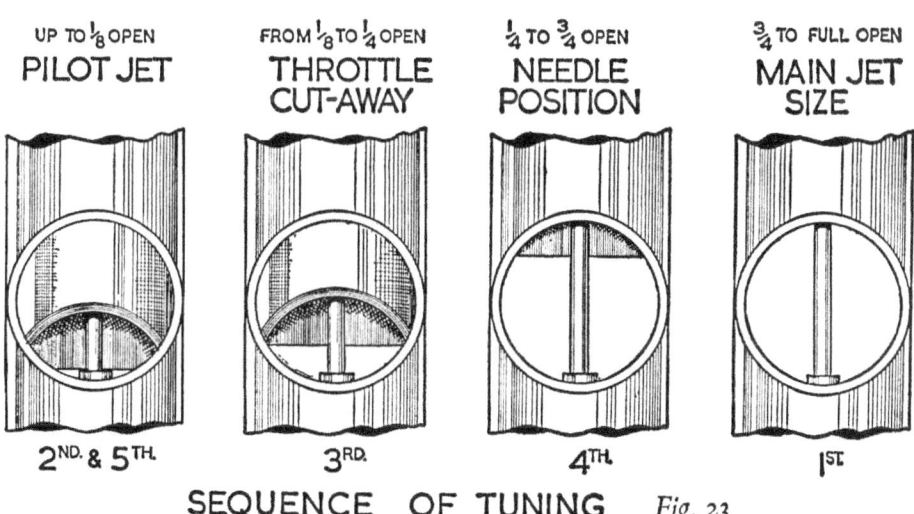

PHASES OF AMAL NEEDLE JET CARBURETTOR THROTTLE OPENINGS

SEQUENCE OF TUNING *Fig. 23*

3. **Throttle cut away - with throttle $\frac{1}{8}$ in. to $\frac{1}{4}$ in. open.** If, as the throttle is opened from the idling position, there is spitting back through the carburettor, slightly richen the pilot mixture adjustment. If this is not effective, return to the original adjustment and fit a throttle slide with a smaller cut away, which will richen the mixture at this throttle opening.

If the engine jerks under load, either the jet needle is too high or a throttle slide with a larger cut away is required.

4. **Jet needle - with throttle $\frac{1}{4}$ in. to $\frac{3}{4}$ in.** The jet needle controls a wide range of throttle opening and the acceleration. Try the needle in a low position and if the acceleration is poor but improves by partial closure of the air slide raise the needle two grooves. If the results are very much better, try lowering the needle one groove and after tests leave it in the groove giving the best results.

If, with the needle in the top groove, the mixture is still too rich the needle jet should be renewed. If the needle has been in use for a very long period, renew it also.

Amal Concentric Type 930 - P11

This engine is fitted with twin Amal 930 right-and left-hand carburettors with concentric float chambers. To dismantle the carburettor, remove the two float-bowl fixing screws allowing the float bowl to be detached from the mixing chamber and the float and hinge pin to be removed. The main and pilot jets are now accessible and can be removed for cleaning.

To remove the throttle slide, needle and air slide, detach the top plate, which is secured to the mixing chamber by two small screws.

Tuning

Carburettor tuning is carried out in a manner similar to that already described although in some cases one carburettor may require a slightly different setting from the other.

With twin carburettors accurate synchronisation is essential, both throttles must open simultaneously and reach the fully open position together.

To set the carburettors, slacken the throttle-stop screws fully and close the twist-grip control. Adjust the cable adjusters so that with the handlebars in the normal position there is slight and equal backlash on each carburettor and as the twist grip is operated the throttle slides begin to lift simultaneously. This can be checked by removing the air filter and placing the fingers inside the carburettor intake as the twist grip is rotated.

To adjust the idling speed, open the twist grip slightly until the engine idles at the required speed then screw in the throttle-stop screws until they just make contact with the throttle slides, holding them in that position. Return the twist grip control to the fully closed position.

Check that both throttle slides are fully lifted when the twist grip is in the fully open position.

When adjusting the pilot-jet mixture strength and idling speed, accuracy can be obtained by disconnecting one plug lead and tuning each cylinder as a single unit. When both leads are connected, the engine speed will increase and if necessary should be reduced by unscrewing each throttle-stop screw equally.

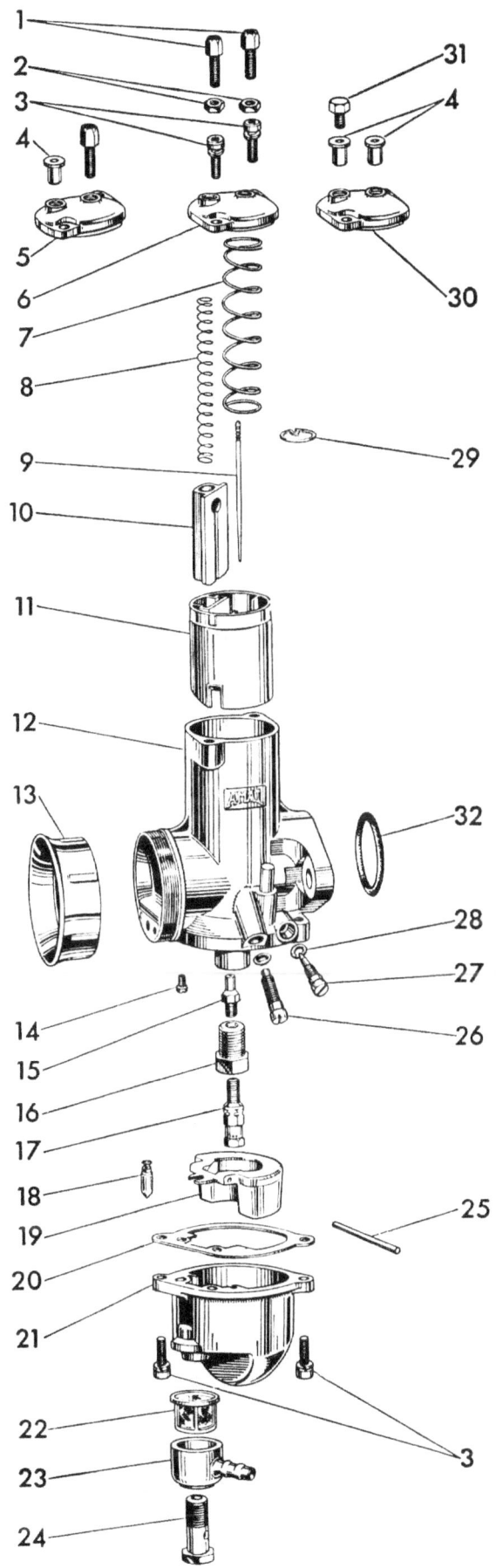

Fig. 24
Amal concentric carburettor

1. Cable adjuster
2. Cable-adjuster locknut
3. Float-chamber and mixing-chamber-top securing screws
4. Cable ferrules
5. Mixing-chamber top for adjuster and ferrule
6. Mixing-chamber top (standard)
7. Throttle-valve spring
8. Air-valve spring
9. Throttle needle
10. Air valve
11. Throttle valve
12. Carburettor body and tickler assembly
13. Air-intake tube
14. Pilot jet
15. Needle jet
16. Jet holder
17. Main jet
18. Float needle
19. Float
20. Float-chamber washer
21. Float-chamber body
22. Filter
23. Banjo union
24. Banjo bolt
25. Float spindle
26. Throttle-stop adjusting screw
27. Pilot-air adjusting screw
28. 'O' Rings
29. Needle clip
30. Mixing-chamber top for two ferrules
31. Plug for mixing-chamber top
32. 'O' ring for flange sealing

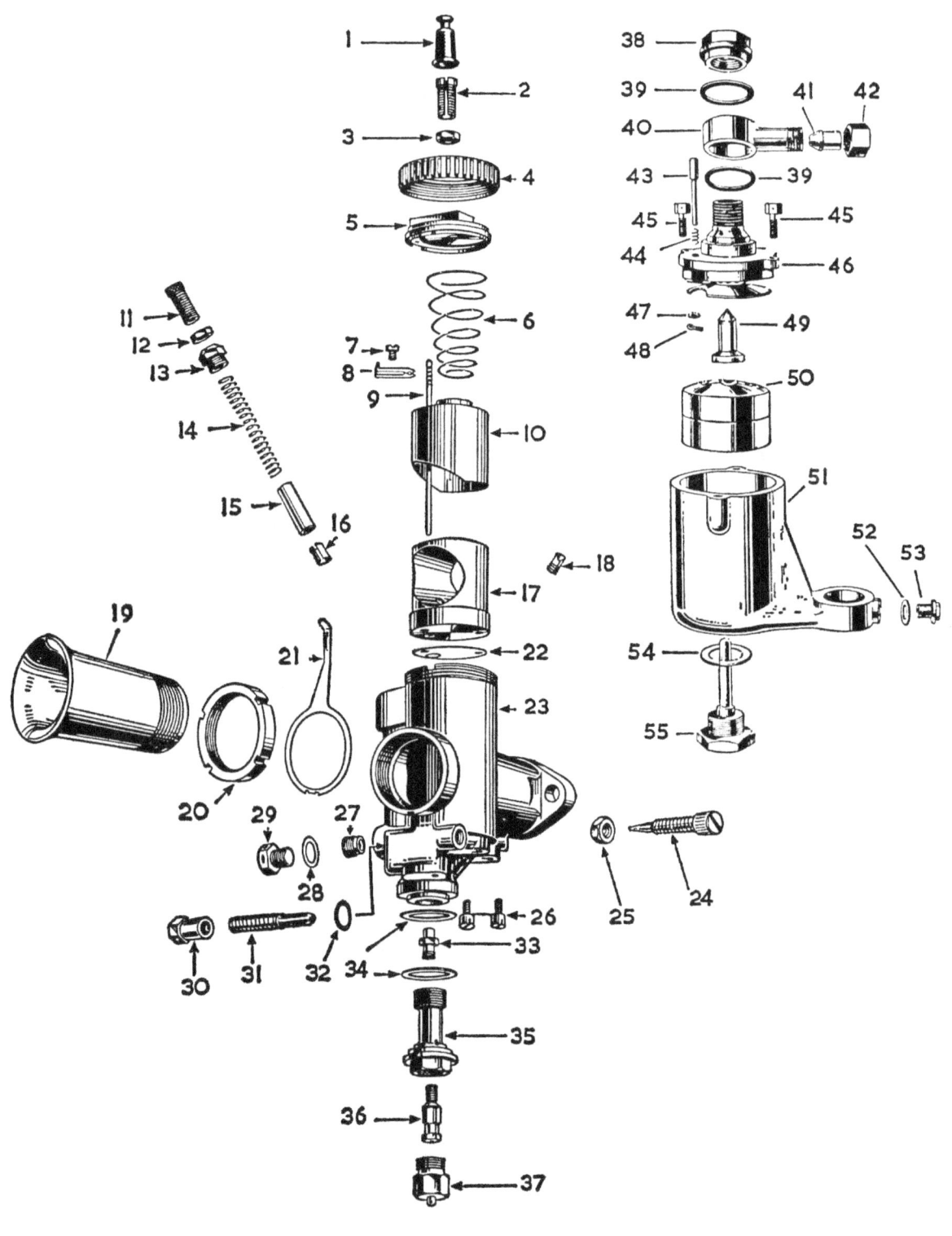

Fig. 25
Amal 5GP2 carburettor

Amal 5GP2 - G85CS

This model is fitted with the Amal 5GP2 carburettor which is designed to obtain the maximum possible power from the engine. To achieve this, the throttle needle has been moved to permit an unrestricted bore at full throttle and to leave a very short tract for the mixture to travel from the needle jet to the choke.

The main jet is accessible when the cap nut at the base of the mixing chamber is removed. The needle jet is screwed into the top of the jet holder. The idling mixture is regulated by the pilot air adjusting screw located in the side of the mixing-chamber body the pilot jet being directly opposite and protected by a small cover nut.

To remove the throttle slide and needle, unscrew the knurled top ring. The needle is secured by a spring clip located in one of the grooves provided for adjustment.

The correct fuel level is $1\frac{5}{16}$ in. below the top-cover joint.

Tuning

The tuning sequence is similar to that already described. The main jet should be the smallest size to give the maximum speed and permit the engine to run at a safe temperature.

When adjusting the pilot jet, take care that the 'tick-over' is not set too slowly, causing "stalling" at small throttle openings or when the throttle is "snapped" open.

The throttle cut-away controls throttle openings from about $\frac{1}{8}$ to just over $\frac{1}{4}$ and if when opening up slowly from this position the exhaust note becomes irregular the throttle should be left in this position and the air lever used to determine whether the mixture is rich or weak. Fit a throttle slide with a larger cut-away if the mixture is rich and with less cut-away if it is weak.

The jet needle controls throttle openings of about $\frac{1}{3}$ to $\frac{7}{8}$ and as the throttle is opened the air lever should be used to determine the mixture strength. By moving the needle securing clip into alternative grooves, the needle can be raised to richen the mixture or lowered to weaken it.

Key to Fig. 25 - Amal 5GP2 carburettor

1. Cable-adjuster sheath
2. Throttle-cable adjuster
3. Locknut
4. Mixing-chamber cap
5. Mixing-chamber top
6. Throttle-valve spring
7. Jet needle-clip screw
8. Jet-needle clip
9. Jet needle
10. Throttle valve
11. Air-valve cable adjuster
12. Locknut
13. Air-barrel top
14. Air-valve spring
15. Air valve
16. Air-valve nipple holder
17. Choke adaptor
18. Spray tube
19. Air tube
20. Air-tube lockring
21. Mixing-chamber cap-lock spring
22. Choke-adaptor washer
23. Mixing-chamber body
24. Pilot-air adjuster
25. Locknut
26. Choke-adaptor fixing screws
27. Air jet
28. Air-jet plug-screw washer
29. Air-jet plug screw
30. Pilot jet-cover nut
31. Pilot jet
32. Pilot jet cover-nut washer
33. Needle jet
34. Banjo washers
35. Jet holder
36. Main jet
37. Jet-holder plug screw
38. Banjo nut
39. Banjo washers
40. Banjo
41. Nipple
42. Union nut
43. Tickler
44. Tickler spring
45. Cover fixing screws
46. Float-chamber cover
47. Tickler washer
48. Tickler cotter
49. Float needle
50. Float
51. Float chamber
52. Plug-screw washer
53. Plug screw
54. Base-plug washer
55. Base plug and guide

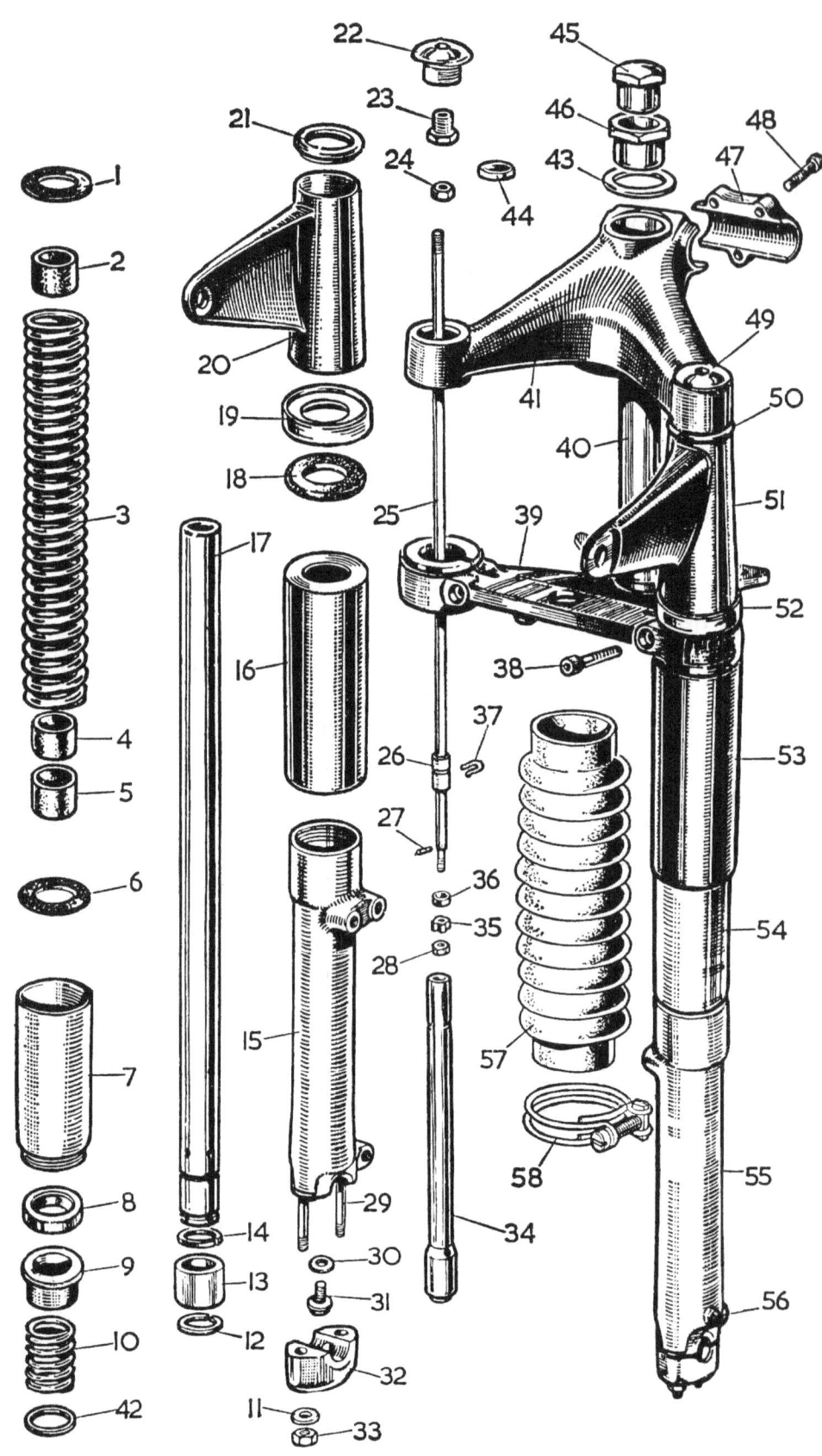

Fig. 26
Teledraulic front forks

Front Forks - all models

The numbers referred to in this section are shown in Fig. 26.

Steering-head adjustment

Do not use a machine with movement in the steering-head bearings as the racking motion that takes place when the machine is being ridden over rough ground and when the front brake is applied will quickly destroy the bearings. To adjust the bearings support the machine by placing a wooden box under each footrest. Release the two Allen screws (38) which pass through the fork crown (39) and clamp the fork tubes.

Slacken off the top nut (45) and tighten the adjusting nut (46) sufficiently to take up the movement, but leaving the forks free to move without friction.

When the adjustment has been made tighten the locknut and the Allen screws. With the machine supported in the manner described try to detect movement by raising the front wheel with one hand, holding the top of the frame and the handlebar lug with the other. Any movement in the bearing will be readily felt.

Key to Fig. 26

1 Leather washer	30 Fibre washer
2 Rubber buffer	31 Bolt
3 Main spring	32 Fork slider cap
4 Rubber buffer	33 Nut
5 Rubber buffer	34 Fork damper tube
6 Leather washer	35 Fork damper-valve seat
7 Extension	36 Fork damper valve
8 Oil seal	37 Clip
9 Top bush	38 Pinch screw
10 Buffer spring	39 Fork crown
11 Plain washer	40 Fork crown stem
12 Circlip	41 Handlebar and steering head lug
13 Steel bottom bush	42 Buffer spring collar
14 Circlip	43 Washer (Not now fitted)
15 Slider	44 Rubber sealing ring
16 Fork cover tube (bottom)	45 Locknut
17 Fork inner tube	46 Fork stem adjusting nut
18 Rubber ring	47 Clip
19 Housing ring	48 Clamp screw
20 Fork cover tube (top right)	49 Bolt
21 Spigot ring	50 Spigot ring
22 Fork inner tube bolt	51 Fork cover tube (top left)
23 Adaptor	52 Housing ring
24 Locknut	53 Fork cover tube (bottom
25 Fork damper rod	54 Fork slider extension
26 Plunger sleeve	55 Fork slider
27 Fork damper-valve stop pin	56 Plug screw with fibre washer
28 Locknut	57 Gaiter for cover tube and extension
29 Stud	58 Clip

Topping-up forks

Apart from maintaining the oil level, the forks do not require individual lubrication. The oil level should be checked every 5,000 miles and topped up as necessary.

Draining the oil

Have a graduated container of not less than 10 fluid oz. available.
Support the front wheel to enable the forks to be fully extended.
Unscrew the top fork-tube bolt (22) to allow air to enter.
Turn the forks on full lock and take out the drain screw (56), allowing the oil to drain into the container. If the level is correct, 6 fluid oz. of oil will drain off leaving ½ fluid oz. in suspense.
Return the drain screw and pour in 6 fluid oz. of S.A.E.20 oil and tighten the top-tube bolt.

Removing forks as a unit

Support the machine with both wheels clear of the ground.
Disconnect the steering-damper plate from the frame.
Disconnect the steering-damper plate from the chassis.
Remove the front wheel and the front mudguard and stay.
Disconnect the speedometer or tachometer, if fitted.
Remove the handlebars and controls, providing some protection for the gas tank.
Detach front-brake cable from brake lever by removing the yoke and the adjuster.
Remove the rubber grommet and unscrew the top bolt (22).
Undo the locking nut (24) and disconnect the damper rod (25).
Remove the dome nut (45) on steering column, support the front wheel and take off the adjusting nut (46). Use a soft-faced mallet to disengage the handlebar lug from the fork tubes. Take care of the bearings. Take away the front-wheel support and remove the forks from the frame.

Refitting forks

When refitting the forks, in the reverse order, remember that a total of 56 steel balls are used for the top and lower steering-head races.

Removing fork slider

With the front wheel clear of the ground, unscrew the top fork-tube bolt and disconnect the damper rod. Release the fork-gaiter clips to move the gaiter and unscrew the fork-slider extension (54) before removing the front wheel and mudguard stays.
The oil seal (8) is a close fit in the slider and if a sharp jerk downwards fails to free it heat the top portion of the slider to facilitate its removal.
Reassembly is in the reverse order, using a length of wire to "fish" up the damper rod. Make good any oil lost during dismantling.
To take out a fork tube, the clamping screw (38) must be released before drifting the tube out of the two top lugs.

Rear Suspension

These are sealed units and are filled with oil during assembly. A grating noise when movement takes place can be eliminated by applying grease to the outside diameter of the unit springs. The cam-ring adjuster, if turned clockwise, will raise the base of the spring to suit varying loads.

To expose springs

To remove the unit, take out the top and lower fixing bolts. Compress the spring by downward pressure to take out the two split collets securing the spring cover. The cover can then be lifted off and the spring removed.

Swinging arm

The bearing for the swinging arm consists of four Silentbloc-type bearings, two bearings being located at each end of the swinging arm. These bearings are a press fit in the arm tubing and can be pressed out if so desired. No attention or lubrication is needed and the bearings are in no way affected by premature wear.

Wheels and Brakes

To remove front wheel

Jack up the front wheel and take out the cable-yoke split pin to disconnect the cable.
Remove brake torque-stay fixing bolt.
Remove the wheel-spindle nut.
Remove the four nuts retaining the slider caps, freeing the wheel from the forks.

Dismantling front hub

The bearings are pre-packed with grease during assembly and provided the hub does not run hot, due to brake binding, further lubrication is not necessary until 10,000 miles have been covered.

Both bearings are a close fit in the hub, which must be heated to extract them and to prevent a loss of the interference fit when the bearings are refitted. Take out the oil-seal collar and prise out the oil seal. Heat the hub around the bearing and drop the wheel onto a flat wooden bench to move the bearing sufficiently to enable it to be driven out with a drift. Take care to ensure that the bearing comes out parallel with its housing. Pull out the bearing spacer, remove the lock ring, which has a **LEFT-HAND THREAD**, and the hub disc and unscrew the bearing sleeve.

Reheat the hub and drift out the remaining bearing.

Reassembling front hub

Heat the right-side of the hub, insert the bearing and press it fully home. Screw home the bearing sleeve. Invert the hub and pack some grease against the bearing. Insert the bearing spacer tube and pack in more grease to the hub.

Heat the hub and press in the other bearing. Fit the hub disc and secure it with the lock ring. Replace the oil-seal collar in the seal using a new seal if the old one is damaged.

Refitting front wheel

Ensure that the torque arm is firmly fixed as this is a vital part of the assembly. Do not overtighten the four nuts for the slider caps.

Removal of rear wheel (G85CS and P11)

Disconnect the rear-brake rod from the lever.
Take out the connecting link from the rear chain.
Remove the torque-stay fixing bolt.
Release both wheel-spindle nuts and pull the wheel clear of the fork ends.
When refitting the connecting link ensure that the closed end of the spring link faces the direction in which the chain moves.

Dismantling rear hub (G85CS)

A roller bearing is used on the sprocket side of the hub and a ball bearing on the opposite side.

The roller bearing is located by a circlip which must be removed.

Take off the bearing-sleeve lock ring and extract the sleeve.

Apply gentle heat around the bearing areas and drift out the bearings, taking care that they emerge parallel with the hub. Reassemble the hub in the reverse sequence, being careful to locate the circlip correctly.

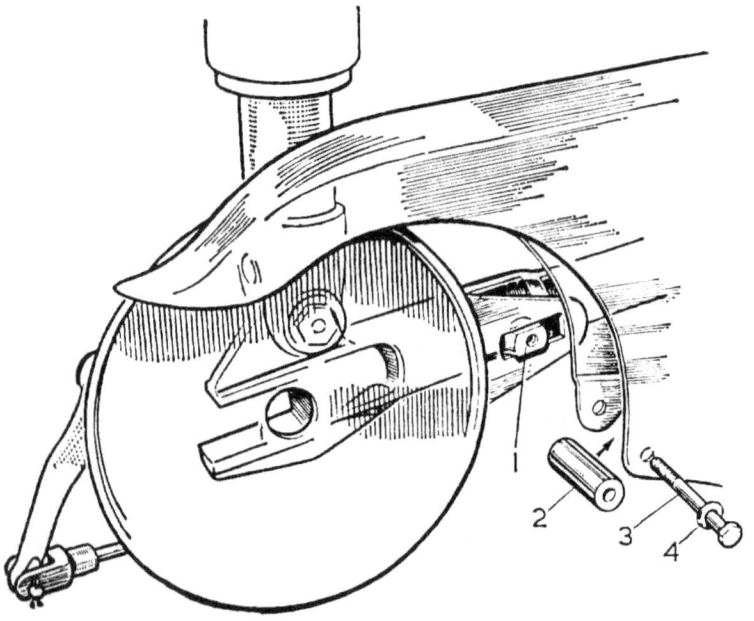

Fig. 28

Rear brake-plate anchorage

1 Brake anchorage boss
2 Spacer
3 Fixing bolt
4 Washer

Removal of rear wheel (G80CS)

The rear wheel is taken out of the frame with the rear sprocket attached to the hub. The method in which the brake plate is attached to the frame is shown in Fig. 27.

Take out the connecting link and disconnect the rear chain.

Remove the rear brake-rod pivot pin.

Take out the bolt passing through the rear chaincase and frame.

Take off the wheel-spindle nut and withdraw the spindle, speedometer drive spacer.

Cant the wheel to the right-hand side of the frame so that the brake plate is clear of its anchorage. The wheel can then be withdrawn.

Brake-shoe adjustment

Adjustment to compensate for wear on the brake linings is made by finger adjustment on the rear-brake rod and by the screwed adjuster on the front-brake cable.

When lining wear takes place after considerable mileage, frequent adjustments reduce the leverage and result in loss of brake efficiency. Provision is made to compensate for this by placing packing washers under the head of the hardened thrust pins used on both brake shoes. The method, shown in Fig. 29, applies to the front-and rear-brake shoes on the G80CS model and the front brake only on the G85CS model, which has a racing-type rear brake with a two-piece lining.

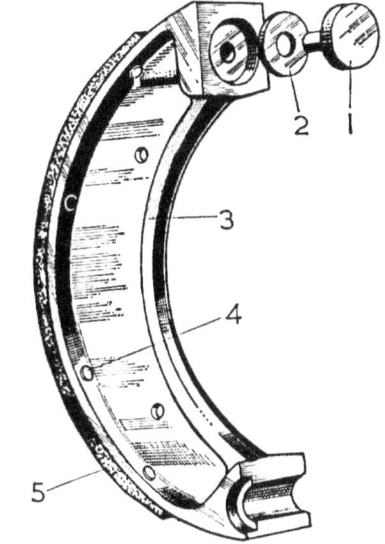

Fig. 29
Brake shoe adjustment
1 Thrust pin 2 Packing washer
3 Brake shoe 4 Rivet
5 Brake lining

Centralising brake shoes

When reassembling, the brake shoes should be centralised. In the case of the front brake, leave the spindle nut loose, pull hard on the brake operating lever and maintain the the pressure until the spindle nut has been firmly tightened. Use the same method for the rear brake, after which it will be possible to adjust the brake closely without binding.

Dismantling rear hub (G80CS)

As there are 17 parts in this rear-hub assembly components should be systematically laid out on the bench during dismantling so that they will be fitted correctly when re-assembling. The order of dismantling is as follows:

Release the bearing adjuster-sleeve lock ring.

Unscrew the adjuster sleeve, which will come away with the speedometer-drive sleeve and the hub-cover disc.

Take out the small washer, oil seal and oil-seal cup.

From the brake side insert a bar through the hub to force out the right-side bearing and the hub central distance piece, leaving in the left-side of the hub the bearing ring, oil seal, washers and circlip.

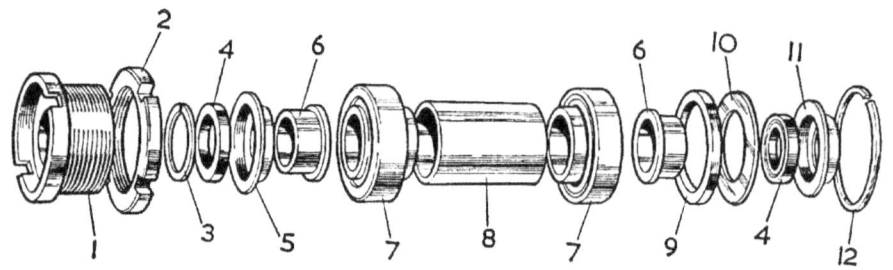

Fig. 29

Rear-hub bearings

1 Bearing adjuster
2 Lock ring
3 Seal retaining ring
4 Seal for bearing
5 Oil-seal cup
6 Oil-seal spacers
7 Taper-roller bearings
8 Bearing spacer
9 Packing washer
10 Seal retaining ring
11 Oil-seal cup
12 Circlip

To remove the remaining bearing sleeve press on the cup washer under the circlip until it is possible to take out the circlip. The outer cup washer, oil seal and spacer will then come out. Press on the bearing ring to extract it from the hub. The order of assembly is shown in Fig. 29.

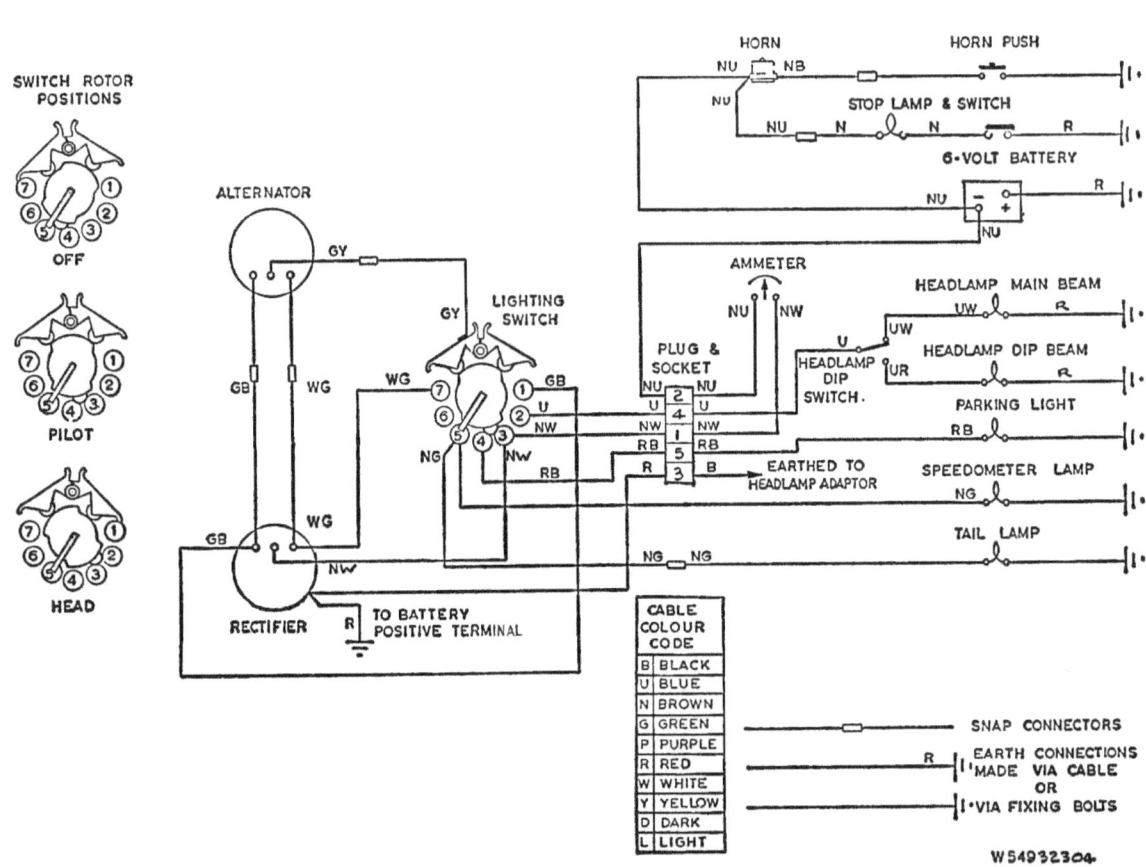

Fig. 30 G85CS and G80CS wiring diagram

Electrical Systems

The magneto type N C I (Lucas 42347E)

Lubrication and adjustment is necessary every 3,000 miles, cleaning at every 5,000 miles. Every 10,000 miles the unit should be serviced by a Lucas service depot.

Lubrication at 3,000 miles

Smear both inside and outside the cam ring with light grease.

Apply a drop of light oil to the contact-breaker pivot taking care to keep oil clear of the contact points.

To remove contact breaker

Take out the hexagon-headed screw from the centre of the contact breaker and pull the assembly from its tapered shaft. When refitting take care to engage the key projection into the keyway in the armature shaft as incorrect location will affect the ignition timing.

Adjustment every 3,000 miles

Remove the contact-breaker cover by inserting a screwdriver in one of the serrations and tapping the end lightly to loosen the cover. Disengage the retaining spring by lifting and unscrewing the cover by hand.

Rotate the engine until the points are fully open and check the gap with a .012 in. feeler gauge. The gauge should be a sliding fit if the gap is correct. To reset the gap see paragraph on checking the ignition timing.

Cleaning every 5,000 to 6,000 miles

Remove the cover and contact breaker and check the points. If they are pitted or burnt restore the surfaces with a fine carborundum stone. Clean the points after with a cloth moistened with gasoline. Check the gap after assembly as already described. Remove the H.T. pick-up and lift the protecting cover. Take out the screws, taking care to avoid dislodging the carbon brush. The brush should move freely and should be cleaned with a gasoline-moistened cloth. If the brush is worn to within $\frac{1}{8}$ in. from the shoulder it needs renewing. Clean the slip-ring track on the armature with a piece of soft fluff-free rag on the end of a lead pencil.

P11 contact breaker

A few drops of light oil applied periodically on the felt wick will lubricate the cam. Apply a few drops behind the base plate to lubricate the auto mechanism. Check the condenser pillar nuts for security.

Type R M 19 alternator (Lucas 54021027)

Lighting equipment is supplied with the G80CS model. The stator is located in the outer portion of the front chaincase, the rotor being mounted on an extension of the drive-side shaft. No routine maintenance is required, other than checking the snap connectors for clean and positive contact.

Rectifier (Lucas 49072A)

This equipment needs no attention other than to ensure that the fixing bolt is tight. The rectifier is located at the rear of the battery carrier. On the P11 model the rectifier is alongside the battery.

Light switch (Lucas 31784D)

On the G80CS the switch is below the rider's seat. It has three positions: 'Off', 'Pilot' and 'Main'. Turn the switch anti-clockwise for the 'Off' position.

Headlamp (Lucas 58829 A/B)

The headlamp, which is a competition type, can be separated from the wiring loom by the detachable-plug assembly under the headlamp shell.

Battery Lucas (MLZ9E) - G80CS

A six-volt system is used with a positive ground, the 12 ampere hour battery being of the lead acid type. New machines are issued with dry charged batteries and electrolyte must be added.

Battery Lucas (PUZ5A) - P11

The P.11 model uses a 12-volt system with a positive ground connection. The battery capacity is 8 ampere/hour rating.

Filling the battery

The specific gravity of the electrolyte must be corrected according to the shade temperature. At 80°F and below add one part of acid (1.835 SG) to 2.8 parts of distilled water to obtain a filling solution with a specific gravity of 1.270 at 60°F.

Where the shade temperature is above 80°F the acid-to-water ratio must be 1.4 to give a specific gravity of 1.270 at 60°F.

Dry-charged batteries are given a four-hour charge at 1.5 to 2.5 amperes.

Battery maintenance

Check the electrolyte level every 14 days and top up with distilled water to the level of the separator guard. If a visible level is not used keep the top of the battery and terminals clean. If the machine is out of service for any length of time recharge the battery every 14 days until each cell is gassing freely. This replaces energy lost during the inactive period.

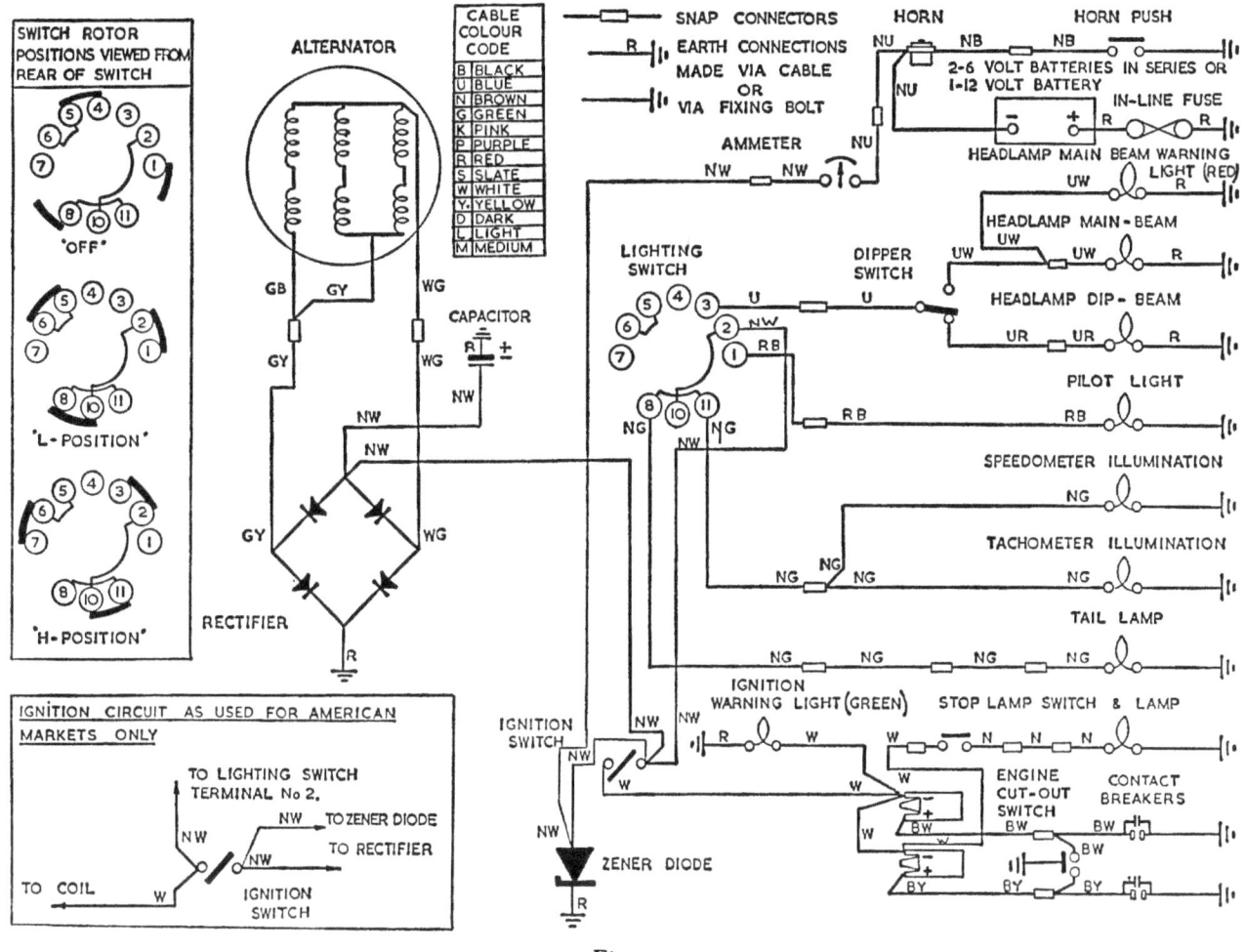

Fig. 31
P11 *wiring diagram*

P11 capacitor-ignition system

The advantage of the capacitor-ignition system over the regular coil-ignition system is that the machine can be used either with or without the battery. Starting the engine and lighting is equally effective with or without the battery, supplementary accessories such as parking lights excepted. Two separate ignition coils are attached to the frame. There are two separate contact breakers and the points for each contact breaker can be adjusted individually for a balanced firing point. The capacitor is attached to the rear frame alongside the battery.

The large-volume capacitor stores energy impulses from the alternator and supplies the ignition coils with sufficient energy for easy starting and high-speed running.

The Zener diode takes care of the voltage output from the alternator and, when in use, the battery is connected across the ammeter to a positive ground connection.

The wiring diagram shows all connections including the rectifier.

Capacitor 2MC

The capacitor is an electrolytic-polarised type and it is important that the correct wiring fittings are made, despite the fact that the capacitor connections are dissimilar in size. The $\frac{3}{16}$ in. connector is the positive ground terminal. The rivet on this connection is marked with red paint. The $\frac{1}{4}$ in. double terminal is the negative.

The capacitor must always be fitted with the terminals DOWNWARDS.

The efficiency of the capacitor can be verified with the use of a fully charged 12-volt battery and voltmeter. Connect the battery across the capacitor terminals, POSITIVE to POSITIVE and NEGATIVE to NEGATIVE, and leave for five minutes.

When the charging period is complete take off the two battery wires and use the 12-volt battery properly connected. An instantaneous reading of 8 volts will indicate that the capacitor is serviceable.

Removing battery

With this equipment, if the battery is removed it is important to insulate the negative battery lead to avoid shorting to the engine or the frame, which would make the capacitor unserviceable. The part number for the capacitor is 541 700 09. A defective capacitor cannot be detected when the battery is in circuit. To check, take off the battery cables and see if the engine will run with full lights.

VELOCEPRESS MANUALS – MOTORCYCLE BY MAKE

AJS 1932-1948 SINGLES & TWINS 250cc THRU 1000cc (BOOK OF)
AJS 1945-1960 SINGLES 350cc & 500cc MODELS 16 & 18 (BOOK OF)
AJS 1955-1965 SINGLES 350cc & 500cc (BOOK OF)
AJS 1957-1966 FACTORY WSM - ALL SINGLES & TWINS
AJS 1959-1969 FACTORY WSM G80CS G85CS & P11 OFF ROAD
ARIEL UP TO 1932 (BOOK OF)
ARIEL 1932-1939 PREWAR MODELS (BOOK OF)
ARIEL 1933-1951 (WORKSHOP MANUAL)
ARIEL 1939-1960 4 STROKE SINGLES (BOOK OF)
ARIEL 1958-1964 LEADER & ARROW FACTORY WSM & PARTS LIST
ARIEL 1958-1964 LEADER & ARROW (BOOK OF)
BMW R26 R27 (1956-1967) FACTORY WORKSHOP MANUAL
BMW R50 R50S R60 R69S (1955-1969) FACTORY WORKSHOP MANUAL
BMW R50/5 R60/5 R75/5 (1969-1973) FACTORY WORKSHOP MANUAL
BRIDGESTONE 90 SERIES FACTORY WSM & PARTS CATALOGUE
BRIDGESTONE 175 SERIES FACTORY WSM & PARTS CATALOGUE
BRIDGESTONE 350 SERIES FACTORY WSM & PARTS CATALOGUES
BSA SERVICE SHEETS MASTER CATALOGUE ALL MODELS 1945-1967
BSA BANTAM D1 TO D7 1948-1966 FACTORY SERVICE SHEETS MANUAL
BSA BANTAM ALL MODELS FROM 1948 ONWARDS (BOOK OF)
BSA BANTAM D14 FACTORY SERVICE MANUAL
BSA DANDY FACTORY WORKSHOP MANUAL (COMPILATION)
BSA SINGLES & V-TWINS UP TO 1926 inc. 1927 SUPPLEMENT (BOOK OF)
BSA SINGLES & V-TWINS UP TO 1930 (BOOK OF)
BSA SINGLES & V-TWINS UP TO 1935 (BOOK OF)
BSA SINGLES & V-TWINS 1936-1939 (BOOK OF)
BSA C10, C11 & C12 1945-1958 FACTORY SERVICE SHEETS MANUAL
BSA OHV & SV SINGLES 250-600cc 1945-1959 (BOOK OF)
BSA C15 & B40 1958-1967 FACTORY SERVICE SHEETS MANUAL
BSA OHV & SV SINGLES 250cc (ONLY) 1954-1970 (BOOK OF)
BSA B31, B32, B33 & B34 1945-60 FACTORY SERVICE SHEETS MANUAL
BSA OHV SINGLES 350 & 500cc 1955-1967 (BOOK OF)
BSA M20, M21 & M33 1945-1963 FACTORY SERVICE SHEETS MANUAL
BSA TWINS A7 & A10 1948-1962 FACTORY SERVICE SHEETS MANUAL
BSA TWINS A7 & A10 1948-1962 (BOOK OF)
BSA TWINS A50 & A65 1962-1965 FACTORY WORKSHOP MANUAL
BSA TWINS A50 & A65 1962-1969 (SECOND BOOK OF)
DOUGLAS 1929-1939 PREWAR ALL MODELS (BOOK OF)
DOUGLAS 1948-1957 POSTWAR ALL MODELS FACTORY SHOP MANUAL
DUCATI 160cc, 250cc & 350cc OHC MODELS FACTORY SHOP MANUAL
HONDA 50cc ALL MODELS UP TO 1970 INC MONKEY & TRAIL (BOOK OF)
HONDA 90cc ALL MODELS UP TO 1966 (BOOK OF)
HONDA TWINS & SINGLES 50cc THRU 305cc 1960-1966 (BOOK OF)
HONDA TWINS ALL MODELS 125cc THRU 450cc UP TO 1968 (BOOK OF)
HONDA C100 50cc SUPER CUB O.H.C. 1959-1962 FACTORY WSM
HONDA C110 50cc SPORT CUB O.H.C. 1960-1962 FACTORY WSM
HONDA 50-65-70-90cc O.H.C. SINGLES 1959-1983 WSM
HONDA 100-125cc SINGLES CB/CD/CL/SL/TL 1970-1984 FACTORY WSM
HONDA 125-150cc TWINS C/CS/CB/CA 1959-1966 FACTORY WSM
HONDA 125-160-175-200cc TWINS 1965-1978 WORKSHOP MANUAL
HONDA 250-305cc TWINS CB/CL 1961-1968 FACTORY WSM
HOHDA 250-350cc TWINS CB/CL/SL 1968-1973 FACTORY WSM
HONDA 250-360cc TWINS CB/CL/CJ 1974-1977 FACTORY WSM
HONDA 350F & 400F 4-CYLINDER 1972-1977 FACTORY WSM
HONDA 450cc TWINS CB 1965-1974 K0 TO K7 WORKSHOP MANUAL
HONDA 500cc & 550cc 4-CYL 1971-1978 FACTORY WORKSHOP MANUAL
HONDA 750cc SHOC 4-CYL 1969-1978 K0~K8 WORKSHOP MANUAL
INDIAN PONYBIKE, BOY RACER & PAPOOSE ILL PARTS LIST & SALES LIT

J.A.P. ENGINES 1927-1952 & MOTORCYCLES 1934-1952 (BOOK OF)
MATCHLESS 1931-1939 ALL MODELS 250cc THRU 990cc (BOOK OF)
MATCHLESS 1945-1956 350 & 500cc SINGLES (BOOK OF)
MATCHLESS 1955-1966 350 & 500cc SINGLES (BOOK OF)
MATCHLESS 1957-1966 FACTORY WSM - ALL SINGLES & TWINS
NEW IMPERIAL ALL SV & OHV FROM 1935 ONWARDS (BOOK OF)
NORTON 1932-1939 PREWAR MODELS (BOOK OF)
NORTON 1932-1947 (BOOK OF)
NORTON 1938-1956 (BOOK OF)
NORTON 1945-1963 MODELS 16H, Big4, ES2, 19 & 50 WSM'S & PARTS
NORTON 1955-1963 MODELS 19, 50 & ES2 (BOOK OF)
NORTON 1948-1970 DOMINATOR TWINS FACTORY WSM'S & PARTS
NORTON 1955-1965 DOMINATOR TWINS (BOOK OF)
NORTON 1960-1970 TWIN CYLINDER FACTORY WORKSHOP MANUAL
NORTON 1970-1975 COMMANDO 850 & 750cc FACTORY WSM
NORTON 1975-1978 MK 3 COMMANDO 850 cc FACTORY WSM
PANTHER 1932-1958 LIGHTWEIGHT MODELS 250 & 350cc (BOOK OF)
PANTHER 1938-1966 HEAVYWEIGHT MODELS 600 & 650cc (BOOK OF)
PENTON-KTM-SACHS 1968-1975 100cc & 125cc WORKSHOP MANUAL
RALEIGH MOTORCYCLES 1919-1933 (BOOK OF)
ROYAL ENFIELD 1934-1946 SINGLES & V TWINS (BOOK OF)
ROYAL ENFIELD 1937-1953 SINGLES & V TWINS (BOOK OF)
ROYAL ENFIELD 1946-1962 SINGLES (BOOK OF)
ROYAL ENFIELD 1948-1962 350cc & 500cc PRE-UNIT BULLET WSM
ROYAL ENFIELD 1948-1963 500cc TWINS FACTORY WORKSHOP MANUAL
ROYAL ENFIELD 1952-1963 700cc TWINS FACTORY WORKSHOP MANUAL
ROYAL ENFIELD 1956-1966 CRUSADER & 350cc NEW BULLET WSM
ROYAL ENFIELD 1958-1966 250cc & 350cc SINGLES (SECOND BOOK OF)
ROYAL ENFIELD 1962-1970 INTERCEPTOR WSM'S & PARTS (Compilation)
RUDGE 1933-1939 (BOOK OF)
SACHS 1968-1975 100cc & 125cc ENGINES WSM & M/CYCLE PARTS LIST
SUNBEAM 1928-1939 (BOOK OF)
SUNBEAM 1946-1957 S7 & S8 (BOOK OF)
SUZUKI 50cc & 80cc UP TO 1966 (BOOK OF)
SUZUKI T10 1963-1967 FACTORY WORKSHOP MANUAL
SUZUKI T20 & T200 1965-1969 FACTORY WORKSHOP MANUAL
SUZUKI TWINS 1962 ONWARDS 125-500cc WORKSHOP MANUAL
TRIUMPH 1935-1949 SINGLES & TWINS (BOOK OF)
TRIUMPH 1937-1961 SINGLES SV & OHV 250cc-600cc + TERRIER & CUB
TRIUMPH 1945-1955 PRE-UNIT 350cc, 500cc & 650cc TWINS WSM No.11
TRIUMPH 1945-1959 TWINS (BOOK OF)
TRIUMPH 1956-1969 TWINS (BOOK OF)
TRIUMPH 1956-1962 PRE-UNIT 500cc & 650cc TWINS WSM No.17
TRIUMPH 1957-1963 UNIT CONSTRUCTION 350-500cc WSM No.4
TRIUMPH 1963-1974 UNIT CONSTRUCTION 350-500cc FACTORY WSM
TRIUMPH 1963-1970 UNIT CONSTRUCTION 650cc FACTORY WSM
TRIUMPH 1968-1974 TRIDENT T150 & T150V FACTORY WSM
TRIUMPH 1971-1973 650cc OIL-IN-FRAME FACTORY WSM
TRIUMPH 1973-1978 750cc BONNEVILLE & TIGER FACTORY WSM
TRIUMPH 1979-1983 750cc T140, TR7 & TR65 FACTORY WSM
VELOCETTE 1925-1970 ALL SINGLES & TWINS (BOOK OF)
VELOCETTE 1933-1952 MOV-MAC-MSS RIGID FRAME FACTORY WSM
VELOCETTE 1953-1960 MAC SPRING FRAME WSM & ILL PARTS LIST
VELOCETTE 1954-1971 MSS-VENOM-THRUXTON-VIPER FACTORY WSM
VILLIERS ENGINE UP TO 1959 INC. 3 WHEELERS (BOOK OF)
VILLIERS ENGINE UP TO 1969 (BOOK OF)
VINCENT 1935-1955 (WORKSHOP MANUAL)
YAMAHA 1961-1967 YA5 & YA6 (WORKSHOP MANUAL & ILL PARTS LIST)
YAMAHA 1971-1972 JT1& JT2 (WORKSHOP MANUAL & ILL PARTS LIST)

VELOCEPRESS MANUALS – SCOOTERS BY MAKE

BSA SUNBEAM SCOOTER WORKSHOP MANUAL 1959-1965
BSA SUNBEAM SCOOTER 1959-1965 (BOOK OF)
LAMBRETTA 1947-1957 ALL 125 & 150cc MODELS (BOOK OF)
LAMBRETTA 1957-1970 LI & TV MODELS (SECOND BOOK OF)
NSU PRIMA 1956-1964 ALL MODELS (BOOK OF)
TRIUMPH TIGRESS SCOOTER WORKSHOP MANUAL 1959-1965
TRIUMPH TIGRESS SCOOTER (BOOK OF)
VESPA 1951-1961 (BOOK OF)
VESPA 1955-1963 125 & 150cc & GS MODELS (SECOND BOOK OF)
VESPA 1955-1968 GS & SS (BOOK OF)
VESPA 1963-1972 90, 125 & 150cc (THIRD BOOK OF)

VELOCEPRESS MANUALS – MOPEDS & MOTORIZED BICYCLES

CYCLEMOTOR (BOOK OF)
NSU QUICKLY 1953-1963 ALL MODELS (BOOK OF)
PUCH MAXI N & S MAINTENANCE & REPAIR (3 MANUAL COMPILATION)
RALEIGH MOPEDS 1960-1969 (BOOK OF)

VELOCEPRESS MANUALS - THREE WHEELER'S

BOND MINICAR THREE WHEELER 1948-1967 (BOOK OF)
BMW ISETTA FACTORY WORKSHOP MANUAL
BSA THREE WHEELER (BOOK OF)
RELIANT REGAL THREE WHEELER 1952-1973 (BOOK OF)
VINTAGE MORGAN THREE WHEELER (BOOK OF)

VELOCEPRESS TECHNICAL BOOKS – MOTORCYCLE

1930'S BRITISH MOTORCYCLE CARBS & ELEC COMPONENTS (BOOK OF)
1930'S BRITISH MOTORCYCLE ENGINES (OVERHAUL & MAINTENANCE)
1930'S BRITISH MOTORCYCLE GEARBOXES & CLUTCHES (BOOK OF)
CATALOG OF BRITISH MOTORCYCLES (1951 MODELS)
LUCAS ELECTRONICS BRITISH M/CYCLES REPAIR & PARTS (1950-1977)
MOTORCYCLE ENGINEERING (P.E. Irving)
MOTORCYCLE ROAD TESTS 1949-1953 (Motor Cycle Magazine UK)
SPEED AND HOW TO OBTAIN IT (Motor Cycle Magazine UK)
TUNING FOR SPEED (P.E. Irving)
WIPAC (COMBO) MANUAL NUMBER 3 + M/CYCLE & SCOOTER MANUAL

VELOCEPRESS MANUALS – AUTOMOBILE BY MAKE

ALFA ROMEO GIULIA WORKSHOP MANUAL 1300 TO 2000cc 1962-1975
ALFA ROMEO GIULIA TECH MANUAL CARBURETED CARS FROM 1962
ALFA ROMEO GIULIA TECH MANUAL FUEL INJECTED CARS FROM 1969
ALFA ROMEO GIULIETTA & GIULIA 750 & 101 SERIES 1955-1965 WSM
AUSTIN-HEALEY SPRITE & MG MIDGET WORKSHOP MANUAL 1958-1971
BMW 600 LIMOUSINE FACTORY WORKSHOP MANUAL
BMW 600 LIMOUSINE OWNERS HAND BOOK & SERVICE MANUAL
BMW 2000 & 2002 1966-1976 WORKSHOP MANUAL
BMW 2500, 2800, 3.0 & BARVARIA WORKSHOP MANUAL
CORVAIR 1960-1969 WORKSHOP MANUAL
CORVETTE V8 1955-1962 WORKSHOP MANUAL
FERRARI HANDBOOK ROAD & RACE CARS (SERVICE/SPECS) 1948-1958
FERRARI 250GT SERVICE & MAINTENANCE by JIM RIFF 1956-1965
FERRARI 250GT & 250GTE FACTORY PARTS AND REPAIR MANUALS
FIAT 500 FACTORY WORKSHOP MANUAL 1957-1973
FIAT 600, 600D & MULTIPLA FACTORY WORKSHOP MANUAL 1955-1969
JAGUAR E-TYPE 3.8 & 4.2 SERIES 1 & 2 WORKSHOP MANUAL
JAGUAR MK 7, 8, 9 & XK120, 140, 150 WORKSHOP MANUAL 1948-1961
MERCEDES-BENZ 280 SERIES 1968-1972
METROPOLITAN FACTORY WORKSHOP MANUAL
MGA & MGB OWNERS HANDBOOK & WORKSHOP MANUAL
MG MIDGET TC, TD, TF & TF1500 WORKSHOP MANUAL
PORSCHE 356 1948-1965 WORKSHOP MANUAL
PORSCHE 911 2.0, 2.2, 2.4 LITRE 1964-1973 WORKSHOP MANUAL
PORSCHE 911 2.7, 3.0, 3.2 LITRE 1973-1989 WORKSHOP MANUAL
PORSCHE 912 WORKSHOP MANUAL
PORSCHE 914/4 & 914/6 1.7, 1.8, 2.0 LITRE 1970-1976 WSM
TRIUMPH TR2, TR3, TR4 1953-1965 WORKSHOP MANUAL
VOLKSWAGEN TRANSPORTER, TRUCKS & WAGONS 1950-1979 WSM
VOLVO 1944-1968 ALL MODELS WORKSHOP MANUAL

VELOCEPRESS TECHNICAL BOOKS - AUTOMOBILE

HOW TO BUILD A FIBERGLASS CAR
HOW TO BUILD A RACING CAR
HOW TO RESTORE THE MODEL 'A' FORD
MASERATI OWNER'S HANDBOOK
PERFORMANCE TUNING THE SUNBEAM TIGER
SOUPING THE VOLKSWAGEN
SOLEX CARBURETORS (EMPHASIS ON UK & EU AUTOMOBILES)
SU CARBURETORS (EMPHASIS ON UK AUTOMOBILES)
WEBER CARBURETORS (EMPHASIS ON ALFA & FIAT)

VELOCEPRESS BOOKS & GUIDES - AUTOMOBILE

COMPLETE CATALOG OF JAPANESE MOTOR VEHICLES
FERRARI 308 SERIES BUYER'S AND OWNER'S GUIDE
FERRARI BROCHURES AND SALES LITERATURE 1968-1989
FERRARI SERIAL NUMBERS PART I - ODD NUMBERS TO 21399
FERRARI SERIAL NUMBERS PART II - EVEN NUMBERS TO 1050
HENRY'S FABULOUS MODEL "A" FORD
MASERATI BROCHURES AND SALES LITERATURE

VELOCEPRESS BOOKS – AUTO RACING

BOOK OF THE 1950 CARRERA PANAMERICANA - MEXICAN ROAD RACE
DIALED IN - THE JAN OPPERMAN STORY
VEDA ORR'S NEW REVISED HOT ROD PICTORIAL
LIFE OF TED HORN – AMERICAN RACING CHAMPION

www.VelocePress.com

www.ingramcontent.com/pod-product-compliance
Lightning Source LLC
Chambersburg PA
CBHW081356230426
43667CB00017B/2849